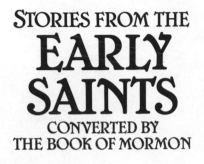

STORIES FROM THE
EARLY SAINTS
CONVERTED BY
THE BOOK OF MORMON

STORIES FROM THE
EARLY SAINTS
CONVERTED BY
THE BOOK OF MORMON

Edited by SUSAN EASTON BLACK

BOOKCRAFT
SALT LAKE CITY, UTAH

The photographs in this book are provided courtesy
of the Historical Department of The Church of
Jesus Christ of Latter-day Saints.

Library of Congress Catalog Card Number: 91–77870

ISBN 0–88494–819–6

First Printing, 1992

Printed in the United States of America

Dedicated to

President Ezra Taft Benson,
prophet of God

Contents

Preface

For more than ten years I have taught Church history and doctrine at Brigham Young University, in Provo, Utah. To enhance my lectures and seminars, I have collected many stories of early Latter-day Saints who were converted to the Church through the Book of Mormon. I kept those stories in my personal files, not thinking I would ever share them in written format. However, in the October 1988 general conference, President Ezra Taft Benson stated: "I challenge our Church writers, teachers, and leaders to tell us more Book of Mormon conversion stories that will strengthen our faith and prepare great missionaries" (5).

When I heard President Benson's challenge, I felt that I must do something more than just add to the files in my office. My third son, John, was following in his older brothers' footsteps in preparing to serve a mission, so I decided to publish these inspiring stories in hopes that they will strengthen John's testimony and the testimonies of others who wish to learn of the powerful conversion process available through reading the Book of Mormon. These stories have touched my heart and increased my faith; may they do the same for you.

I have selected stories from the lives of Saints who joined the Church during its beginnings and knew the Prophet Joseph Smith. I have found that their experiences with the Book of Mormon can be grouped in three clearly defined phases. The first phase is an anticipation of the coming forth of the Book of Mormon. Many early Saints were aware through the gifts of the Spirit that truth was soon to be restored. The second phase is their immediate recognition of the spiritual value of the Book of Mormon. Although some members, such as Brigham Young, spent as much as two years in detailed study of the Book of Mormon before seeking Church membership, each experienced a confirming reaction of joy at reading the new witness for Christ. The final stage is one of sharing. These worthy Saints proclaimed the teachings of the Book of Mormon to friend and foe alike. They defended it from all attacks and testified of its truthfulness despite abuse and persecution. Their recorded testimonies reflect their individual life-styles and where this is practical the original spelling and punctuation have been retained.

These three phases of testimony of the Book of Mormon are also frequently apparent in the Church today. Many converts tell of their search for the fulness of the gospel. Upon reading the Book of Mormon, they recognize that they have found truth. As their testimonies grow, they bear a strong witness of the Book of Mormon's sacred significance and are often placed in a position of defending that witness. Their faithful defense links them to the Prophet Joseph Smith and the early Latter-day Saints who knew and loved him.

I wish to link myself with those of you who are willing to stand and testify of the truthfulness of the Book of Mormon. I have read and studied the Book of Mormon; I have pondered, prayed, and fasted concerning it. I have sought since my youth to know and understand its contents. Day after day I have searched it as an earnest inquirer after truth.

I have found truth! I have discovered my greatest find, truly my pearl of great price. I testify that the Book of Mormon is a powerful, profound witness that Jesus is the Christ, the Son of the Eternal God.

Acknowledgments

I express my appreciation to Becca Wahlquist for sharing with me her research and editing talents. Her suggestions and expertise enhanced this compilation. Shirley Warren was most helpful in the final preparation of the text. Dr. Milton V. Backman, Jr.'s, compilation of writings of early Latter-day Saints proved invaluable in enabling me to place the conversion stories in context with other significant historical events.

Many research materials used in this compilation were obtained by permission from the Historical Department of The Church of Jesus Christ of Latter-day Saints and the Special Collections and Manuscripts room in the Harold B. Lee Library at Brigham Young University. The able staffs at these libraries provided valuable assistance.

My husband, Harvey, and my sons, Brian, Todd, and John, have encouraged me to pursue this compilation. Finally, I want to thank those who attended my classes and lectures and constantly encouraged me to share stories of faith. May their testimonies of the Book of Mormon continue to grow and their lives be enriched by the fulness of its gospel message.

1

Knowing by the Spirit

The ancient prophets of Israel and the Americas were not alone in their foreknowledge of the coming forth of the Book of Mormon. As the restoration of the fulness of the gospel grew near, many valiant men and women anticipated with certainty the approaching event. They were blessed with an abundance of spiritual gifts that foretold the impending good news. Many early Latter-day Saints were prepared for the Book of Mormon through revelations, visions, dreams, and interpretation of dreams. Angels and heavenly manifestations emphasized the promise of restored truth.

Stories of the heavenly preparation of sincere individuals to receive the Book of Mormon strengthen our faith and testimony of this divine scripture. A brief accounting of the Spirit of God at work in their lives illustrates that many of the early Saints were prepared for the coming forth of the Book of Mormon. Their spiritual awakening leads us to conclude that the heavens were opened so that disciples could receive further light and truth.

Asael Smith

"He Had Long Known"

Asael Smith, grandfather of the Prophet Joseph Smith, trusted in the Lord. For his unwavering faith in God he was blessed with a revelation which foretold that the Lord would "raise up some branch of his family to be a great benefit to mankind" (George A. Smith 2). In the fall of 1828, Joseph Smith, Sr., wrote to Asael, sharing portions of the remarkable visions seen by Asael's young grandson, Joseph, Jr. The aging grandfather recognized the heavenly visions as fulfilling his own revelation. He lived long enough to know that his grandson's translation of the gold plates would greatly benefit the human race.

In 1830, as Asael neared the close of his life, Joseph Smith, Sr., traveled to his bedside in St. Lawrence County, New York, and presented him with a copy of the Book of Mormon: "Father received with gladness that which Joseph communicated and remarked that he had always expected that something would appear to make known the true gospel" (Lucy Mack Smith, *Biographical Sketches* 155).

Another grandson, George A. Smith, left a glimpse of Asael's focus during his final months: "My grandfather Asael fully believed the Book of Mormon, which he read nearly through, although in his eighty-eighth year, without the aid of glasses" (2). Regarding the coming forth of the Book of Mormon, Asael predicted that there would be a prophet raised up. Joseph Smith, Jr., said of Asael, "My grandfather . . . declared that I was the very Prophet that he had long known would come in his family." (*History of the Church* 2:443.)

Joseph Smith, Sr.

"Wisdom and Understanding"

In 1811 Joseph Smith, Sr., had two distinct visions that prophesied the coming forth of the Book of Mormon. In the first vision he saw himself traveling in an open, barren field of dead timber, in which a "most death-like silence prevailed." Father Smith soon noticed that he was not alone on his journey, for near his side was an attendant spirit. He inquired of the spirit why he had been sent to such a dismal location. The spirit answered: " 'This field is the world, which now lieth inanimate and dumb, in regard to the true religion, or plan of salvation; . . . you will find on a certain log a box, the contents of which, if you eat thereof, will make you wise, and give unto you wisdom and understanding.' " (Qtd. in Lucy Mack Smith, *History of Joseph Smith* 47.)

This vision served to prepare Father Smith for the truth to be found in the stone box deposited in the Hill Cumorah (see Joseph Smith—History 1:51).

In the second vision Joseph Smith, Sr., saw himself entering a path: "When I had traveled a little way in it, I beheld a . . . very pleasant valley, in which stood a tree such as I had never seen before." This symbolic tree, like that shown to Father Lehi, "bore a kind of fruit . . . as white as snow, or, if possible, whiter." (Compare 1 Nephi 8:11.) Like Lehi, Father Smith approached the tree and began to eat of the white fruit, finding it "delicious beyond description." His family soon joined him at the tree: "The more we ate, the more we seemed to desire, until we even got down upon our knees and scooped it up, eating it by double handfuls." (Qtd. in Lucy Mack Smith, *History of Joseph Smith* 48-50.) This vision portrayed the future joy the Smith family would have because of their acceptance of restored truths contained in the Book of Mormon.

Lucy Mack Smith

"The Breath of Heaven"

When her husband stopped attending the Methodist meetings in Tunbridge, Vermont, Lucy Smith was concerned. Feeling a need for divine assistance, she went into a grove and prayed to the Lord on behalf of her husband. She desired that his heart would soften and that he would become more inclined to accept the churches of his day. After praying for some time in the grove and not receiving an answer, Lucy returned to her home.

That night she dreamed that she saw herself in a beautiful meadow. In the meadow she viewed a clear stream of water and two majestic, towering trees, one of which was encircled by a bright light. Soon a gentle breeze began to blow through the trees, and the brightly lighted one seemed to express joy and happiness in its motions. Lucy wrote, "If it had been an intelligent creature, it could not have conveyed, by the power of language, the idea of joy and gratitude as perfectly as it did." At the close of this dream, Lucy sought an interpretation from the Lord:

> And the interpretation given me was, that these [trees] personated my husband and his oldest brother, Jesse Smith; that the stubborn and unyielding tree was like Jesse; that the other, more pliant and flexible, was like Joseph, my husband; that the breath of heaven, which passed over them, was the pure and undefiled gospel of the Son of God, which gospel Jesse would always resist, but which Joseph, when he was more advanced in life, would hear and receive with his whole heart, and rejoice therein. (*History of Joseph Smith* 44-45.)

"The Most Profound Attention"

The angel Moroni conducted many interviews with Joseph Smith between 1823 and 1827. Joseph often shared the substance of these angelic discussions with his family, informing them of "the great and glorious things which God had manifested to him through the angel" (Lucy Mack Smith, *History of Joseph Smith* 82). From the time that his brother Alvin encouraged family members to finish their day's labor so that all might listen to Joseph, the family gathered nightly to hear him. Lucy recorded:

> From this time forth, Joseph continued to receive instructions from the Lord, and we continued to get the children together every evening for the purpose of listening while he gave us a relation of the same. I presume our family presented an aspect as singular as any that ever lived upon the face of the earth—all seated in a circle, father, mother, sons and daughters, and giving the most profound attention to a boy, eighteen years of age, who had never read the Bible through in his life. (*History of Joseph Smith* 82.)

Mother Smith rejoiced in her son's reports of "the ancient inhabitants of this continent." She wrote of his convincing narrative, "This he would do with as much ease, seemingly, as if he had spent his whole life among them." (*History of Joseph Smith* 83.)

Zera Pulsipher

"That Glorious Day Is Drawing Nigh"

When Zera Pulsipher was twenty-one years old, he married a very "agreeable companion and lived with her about one year when she died, leaving [him] one child" (3). For weeks after his beloved wife's death, Zera remained very anxious about her eternal condition, until one night when she appeared and comforted him:

> Consequently in answer to my desires in a few weeks she came to me in vision and appearing natural looked pleasant as she ever did and sat by my side and assisted me in singing a hymn—beginning thus: "That glorious day is drawing nigh when Zions Light Shall Shine." This she did with a seeming composure. This vision took away all the anxiety of my mind concerning her in as much as she seemed to enjoy herself well. (3.)

This event occurred about ten years before the restoration of the gospel. During the intervening years, Zera served as a Protestant minister. It was not until he was introduced to the Book of Mormon in 1831 that he realized the meaning of the hymn that he had sung with his departed wife and the importance of the message, "That glorious day is drawing nigh." As he pondered the teachings of the Book of Mormon, a further angelic vision confirmed its truthfulness. He later recorded:

> I think about the seventh day as I was threshing in my barn with doors shut, all at once there seemed to be a ray of light from heaven which caused me to stop work for a short time, but soon began it again. Then in a few minutes another light came over my head which caused me to look

up. I thought I saw the angels with the Book of Mormon in their hands in the attitude of showing it to me and saying "this is the great revelation of the last days in which all things spoken of by the prophets must be fulfilled." (5.)

Zera was so moved by this vision that he gathered together his parishioners and informed them of it and of his desire to join with the Saints of God. His testimony was so powerful in its conviction and witness of the divinity of the Book of Mormon that on 11 January 1832 Zera and a large number of his congregation were baptized.

Wilford Woodruff

"The Pure Gospel of Jesus Christ"

On 29 December 1833, two Mormon elders visited the home of Wilford Woodruff. They informed his sister-in-law of a religious meeting that would soon commence in the schoolhouse. When Wilford arrived home and was told of the meeting, he made quick preparations to attend:

> I immediately turned out my horses and started for the schoolhouse without waiting for supper. On my way I prayed most sincerely that the Lord would give me His spirit, and that if these men were the servants of God I might know it, and that my heart might be prepared to receive the divine message they had to deliver. (Qtd. in Cowley 33.)

When Wilford entered the schoolhouse, he found it overcrowded with his friends and neighbors. He climbed on top of a writing desk so that he "could see and hear everything that took place." As the meeting progressed, Wilford recorded, "the spirit of the Lord rested upon me and bore witness that [Zera Pulsipher] was a servant of God." After hearing Elder Pulsipher's testimony of the Prophet Joseph Smith and the divine authenticity of the Book of Mormon, Wilford arose:

> Almost instantly I found myself upon my feet. The spirit of the Lord urged me to bear testimony to the truth of the

message delivered by these elders. I exhorted my neighbors and friends not to oppose these men; for they were the true servants of God. They had preached to us that night the pure gospel of Jesus Christ. (Qtd. in Cowley 33.)

Wilford began to read the Book of Mormon. "As I did so," he wrote, "the spirit bore witness that the record which it contained was true" (qtd. in Cowley 34).

Neighbors in Mendon, New York

"A Noise like the Rushing Wind"

On the night of 22 September 1827, young Joseph Smith climbed the Hill Cumorah and received the gold plates. The same night in the adjacent town of Mendon, New York, neighbors gathered to view wonders in the sky. One neighbor, Vilate Kimball, remembered detailed events of the heavenly wonders. She wrote that she and her husband, Heber C. Kimball, had already retired to bed and were awakened by John Greene, who was desirous that they see the sights in the heavens. Vilate wrote of their astonishment at the scenes that passed before their eyes: "We looked to the eastern horizon, and beheld a white smoke arise towards the heavens. As it ascended, it formed into a belt, and made a noise like the rushing wind, and continued southwest, forming a regular bow, dipping in the western horizon." (Qtd. in Tullidge 107.)

This bow grew larger, stretching into transparency, and soon even stranger sights appeared. Within the bow an army moved, as Vilate described, "commencing from the east and marching to the west. They continued moving in platoons, and walked so close the rear ranks trod in the steps of their file leaders, until the whole bow was literally crowded with soldiers." (Qtd. in Tullidge 107-8.)

Vilate claimed that she and her neighbors saw swords, muskets, bayonets, and uniforms, some including caps and feathers. They even heard "the clashing and jingling of their instruments of war." However, what most amazed this small neighborhood gathering was the unusual order exhibited by the entire army: "When the foremost man stepped, every man stepped at the same time." The gathering of neighbors gazed upon the strange and wondrous scene "for hours, until it began to disappear." (Qtd. in Tullidge 108.)

Frightened by what she had seen, Vilate exclaimed, "What does all this mean?" Father Young answered, "Why it is one of the signs of the coming of the Son of Man." (Qtd. in Tullidge 109.) After learning of the advent of the Book of Mormon, the manifestation's meaning became more clear, and they joined the Church in 1832.

Mary Musselman Whitmer

"Unexpressible Joy and Satisfaction"

Mary Whitmer, wife of Peter Whitmer, Sr., claimed that she was privileged to see the Book of Mormon plates prior to Joseph's completion of their translation. She believed that this privilege was given her because during the translation process she had fed and sheltered Joseph Smith; his wife, Emma; and Oliver Cowdery. Mary explained that while near her and her husband's log cabin in Fayette, New York, an angel appeared to her. John C. Whitmer, a grandson, reported that he heard his grandmother tell of this event on several occasions. He describes her experience:

> She met a stranger carrying something on his back that looked like a knapsack. At first she was a little afraid of him, but when he spoke to her in a kind, friendly tone and began to explain to her the nature of the work which was going on in her house, she was filled with unexpressible joy and satisfaction. He then untied his knapsack and showed her a bundle of plates, which in size and appearance corresponded with the description subsequently given by the witnesses to the Book of Mormon. This strange person turned the leaves of the book of plates over, leaf after leaf, and also showed her the engravings upon them; after which he told her to be patient and faithful in bearing her burden a little longer, promising that if she would do so, she should be blessed; and her reward would be sure, if she proved faithful to the end. The personage then sud-

denly vanished with the plates, and where he went, she could not tell. (Qtd. in Jenson 1:283.)

John Taylor

"A Message to the Nations"

By age fourteen, John Taylor had united with the Methodist society in Liverpool, England, and by age seventeen was recognized as a local preacher. During his youthful religious awakening, he was known to have said to a fellow Methodist, "I have a strong impression on my mind, that I have to go to America to preach the gospel!" (Qtd. in Roberts 28.) The impression he received was so strong that John yearned to leave the British Isles. This yearning was coupled with an earlier vision in which he had seen "an angel in the heavens, holding a trumpet to his mouth, sounding a message to the nations" (Roberts 28). These heavenly manifestations prepared him to leave England in search of greater eternal truths.

John migrated to America and by 1832 had become a Methodist minister in Toronto, Canada. From his own words, we learn that he preached "the leading doctrines of the Christian religion, rather than the peculiar dogmas of Methodism" (qtd. in Roberts 30). His nonconformist approach eventually led to his detachment from the Methodist society and to his earnest prayers for knowledge of a true church of Christ.

His quest was answered through Elder Parley P. Pratt. At first John responded rather coolly to Elder Pratt and his message (he wanted to exercise caution), but later he felt desirous to diligently investigate the matter. At a gathering of gospel seekers in Canada, John asked, "Now, where is our Philip? Where is our receiving the Word with joy, and being baptized *when we believed?* Where is our Peter and John? Our apostles? Where is our Holy Ghost by the laying on of hands?" (Qtd. in Pratt 119.) In answer to this series of questions, on three consecutive evenings Elder Pratt delivered the restored gospel message, affirming his apostolic calling and his authority to act in the name of God. After having written down eight of Parley's sermons, comparing them with the Bible, and after having investigated the Book of Mormon and the Doctrine and Covenants, John Taylor joined the Church.

Oliver Granger

"A True Record of Great Worth"

Oliver Granger acquired a copy of the Book of Mormon a few months after its publication. This volume led to an unexpected angelic visitation. The same angel Moroni who had appeared to the Prophet Joseph Smith also appeared to Oliver in a heavenly vision to testify to the divinity of the Book of Mormon. Oliver recounted this vision to his daughter, Sarah Granger Kimball, who later wrote: "My father was told by a person who said his name was Moroni, that the Book of Mormon, about which his mind was exercised, was a true record of great worth" (qtd. in Crocheron 24). Moroni instructed Oliver to testify of the truthfulness of the Book of Mormon and prophesied that if he would so testify, he "should hereafter be ordained to preach the everlasting Gospel to the children of men" (Crocheron 24).

The angel instructed Oliver to offer a kneeling prayer. As he did so, "Moroni and another personage knelt with him by the bedside. Moroni repeated words and instructed (Oliver) to repeat them after him." (Crocheron 24.)

David Foote

"As It Was Anciently"

By 1830, David Foote had been selected to lead a Methodist Bible class in Dryden, New York, because of his extensive personal study of the Bible. This study led to his dissatisfaction with the Methodist creed and with all other Christian sects of his day. He actively sought to find a true church of Christ, one which contained the organization and purpose established by the Apostles of Jesus Christ as found in the Bible. During his search David had a vision in which he was told that "the true church of Christ would soon be established on earth as it was anciently" (Jenson 1:374).

In the spring of 1830, David borrowed a Book of Mormon from a neighbor. He read the book carefully before testifying that "it was a true record" (Jenson 1:374). In the fall of 1833, Elder John Murdock baptized David. The new convert rejoiced in the knowledge that he had found the true Church of Christ through reading the Book of Mormon.

Warren Foote

"A True Record"

David's son, Warren Foote, followed the example of his father. He was prepared to accept the Book of Mormon as the word of God through his thirst for learning and his delight in reading the Bible. He had been privileged to be educated in all branches of learning taught in the New York schools. He wrote, "I delighted in reading history, but as books were scarce at that time, I read the Bible and became so interested in it, that I read it from Genesis to Revelations three times before I was sixteen years old" (qtd. in Jenson 1:376).

As a result of his great interest in the Bible, Warren attended the Presbyterian Sunday School. In Sunday School he was required to memorize ten verses from the New Testament each week. His growing familiarity with the New Testament caused him to wonder "why there [were] no Apostles, Prophets or spiritual gifts in the churches now, as well as in ancient days." The absence of a church founded on the ancient organization led him to wish that he had "lived in the days of Jesus, and been one of His disciples." He later explained:

> I had no faith in the religious teachings of the various sects, and their revivals and shouting meetings, made no serious impressions on my mind. I could not believe that the Church of Christ was divided into creeds and sects, and I resolved that I would not have anything to do with any of them, but frequently prayed to the Lord in secret to guide me in the right way. (Qtd. in Jenson 1:376.)

When his father, David Foote, borrowed a copy of the Book of Mormon from a neighbor in the spring of 1830, Warren read it. He carefully compared the book with the Bible, and "believed it to be a true record" (qtd. in Jenson 1:376). His intense personal study and comparison led to his baptism on 24 March 1842 by Daniel A. Miller.

Lois Huntington Cutler

"She Was the First to Believe"

Apostle David W. Patten was invited to preach the gospel in the home of Alpheus Cutler near Orleans, New York. Lois Cutler, Alpheus's daughter, listened to Elder Patten's sermon from her sickbed. She had been very ill throughout that winter and had grown weaker and thinner each day. As she listened, Elder Patten spoke of the restoration of the gospel and of the stick of Judah and the stick of Joseph. He held a Bible in one hand and a Book of Mormon in the other and clapped the two books together, declaring, "And they shall be one in the Lord's hands" (Fletcher and Fletcher 12).

To the surprise of those present, Lois clapped her pale hands together and said, "And I believe it." Following her display of faith, she asked Elder Patten to give her a healing blessing. When the blessing ended, Lois got out of bed and walked about the room as if she had never been sick. She told all in her home that "she had been healed by the power of God" (Fletcher and Fletcher 13).

Naturally, the news of Lois's miraculous recovery spread throughout the neighborhood. Many began to listen to Elder Patten, and soon eighteen residents of Orleans joined the Cutlers in requesting baptism. As these individuals neared the baptismal waters, Lois was surprised to hear the officiator say, "The Spirit tells me that Lois is the first to be baptized and if any of you wish to know the reason why, it is because she was the first to believe" (Fletcher and Fletcher 12-13).

Sarah DeArman Pea Rich

"I Was Truly Astonished"

In the summer of 1835, two Mormon Elders preached in Lookinglass Prairie, Illinois. They told of a modern prophet on the earth and his translation of an ancient scripture. Listening to their sermons were seventeen-year-old Sarah Pea and her father. When the Elders completed their sermons, they were invited by Sarah's father to dine with the Pea family. Sarah related:

After supper was over a number of neighbors gathered, to hear these strange men talk. Feeling anxious to see the *Book of Mormon* they told us about, I asked one of the elders if I could see the book, and I asked the company to excuse me for the evening. I retired to my room and spent the rest of that evening and most of night reading it. I was truly astonished at its contents. The book left an impression on my mind never to be forgotten. It appeared to be open before my eyes for weeks afterwards. (Qtd. in John Henry Evans 38.)

The next day when the missionaries left for Ohio, they took with them their copy of the Book of Mormon. Sarah's family believed they would never again see the book or the missionaries.

However, six weeks later Sarah had a dream concerning the missionaries: "I dreamed on Friday night that they would come to our house the next evening, just as the sun was going down, and they would first come in sight at the end of a long lane in front of the house." Sarah was so sure of her dream that she asked her father to come home early that afternoon from a neighboring town. Her father asked, "Why are you so particular? Is your young man coming?" To his teasing, Sarah responded, "No, father, but those two Mormon elders will be here to-night." Her father asked if she had received word from them. Sarah replied, "No, but I dreamed last night they would be here, and I feel sure it will be so." Sarah later explained:

Father said I must be crazy, for those men were hundreds of miles away. But I insisted: "Father, hurry home this evening, for I am sure they will come." He only laughed, and he and mother went off to town. Then I said to my sister, "Let's prepare, for those men will surely be here." (Qtd. in John Henry Evans 39.)

Just as the sun was setting, the missionaries arrived at Sarah's home. As Sarah explained her dream that anticipated their coming, the missionaries told her, "We had a dream that we were to return here and baptize you and build up a church in this region." She asked the Elders to sit inside the house, then returned to the porch to wait for her parents. She related:

In a very short time my father and mother drove into the

yard. As I was standing on the porch, my father said to me, "Well, Sarah, where are your Mormon elders?" I told him they were in the house, at the same time they stepped out on the porch, to meet him. Father was struck with astonishment. (Qtd. in John Henry Evans 39-40.)

The Elders stayed that night with the family and again discussed the coming forth of the Book of Mormon. They remained in the area until they had built up a congregation of over seventy members, including Sarah, her father, her mother, and her sister.

2

A Short, Powerful Witness

Interest in acquiring the Book of Mormon grew so rapidly that when "calls were made for the Book of Mormon . . . there were none on hand to supply the demand" (Robinson). The need had grown because converts were spreading the word about the book—converts like William Huntington, who had read the Book of Mormon and believed it "with all his heart and preached it almost every day, to his neighbors and everybody he could see, or had the privilege to chat with" (Jenson 1:369). Such enthusiasm for sacred truths spread the prophetic words of the Book of Mormon throughout the United States, Canada, and the British Isles during Joseph Smith's lifetime. As eager converts found peace and hope of eternal joy within the pages of this new scripture, many recorded their gratitude and testimony. The following vignettes strengthen our faith by focusing us on the centrality of the Book of Mormon as a key to conversion.

Joseph Smith, Jr.

"The Most Correct of Any Book"

On Sunday, 28 November 1841, Joseph Smith spent the

day in council with the Quorum of the Twelve Apostles at the home of Brigham Young. He spoke to them about the vital scriptural message of the Book of Mormon: "I told the brethren that the Book of Mormon was the most correct of any book on earth, and the *keystone of our religion*, and a man would get nearer to God by abiding by its precepts, than by any other book" (*History of the Church* 4:461, emphasis added).

The Prophet's reference to the Book of Mormon as the "keystone of our religion" places it in a central position. Without the keystone at the top of a Roman archway, the entire structure would fall; so, too, does the Book of Mormon fortify The Church of Jesus Christ of Latter-day Saints. Joseph's statement underscores his testimony that the Book of Mormon provides the strength central to the restored gospel of Christ.

"It Is Truth"

From his youth in Palmyra to his manhood in Nauvoo, Joseph Smith testified powerfully and unwaveringly of the origin and contents of the Book of Mormon. His forceful words comforted his closest associates and swayed his most determined opponents. He neither modified, mitigated, nor varied from his earliest pronouncement that God had called him to translate a scriptural witness of Christ that contained the fulness of the gospel.

In a priesthood meeting held in Kirtland, Ohio, Joseph likened the Book of Mormon to a mustard seed. A seed has a small beginning, yet upon achieving its potential can become a majestic and towering tree. He explained:

> Take the Book of Mormon. . . . Like the mustard seed, [it] becomes the greatest of all herbs. And it is truth, and it has sprouted and come forth out of the earth, and righteousness begins to look down from heaven, and God is sending down His powers, gifts and angels, to lodge in the branches thereof. (*Teachings of the Prophet Joseph Smith* 98.)

Joseph treasured the Book of Mormon and knew that it would influence generations as it spread like a wind-blown seed to flower in all nations. He sowed the seeds of knowledge of the Book of Mormon throughout his lifetime as he testified of its validity.

The Three Witnesses

"We . . . Have Seen the Plates"

While translating, Joseph and Oliver learned from the book of Ether that three witnesses would be shown the plates "by the power of God; wherefore they shall know of a surety that these things are true" (Ether 5:3). Martin Harris, David Whitmer, and Oliver Cowdery desired to be the chosen witnesses. Their request was granted because of their faith. Their testimony is printed in the prefatory pages of the Book of Mormon:

> Be it known unto all nations, kindreds, tongues, and people, unto whom this work shall come: That we, through the grace of God the Father, and our Lord Jesus Christ, have seen the plates which contain this record, which is a record of the people of Nephi, and also of the Lamanites, their brethren, and also of the people of Jared, who came from the tower of which hath been spoken. And we also know that they have been translated by the gift and power of God, for his voice hath declared it unto us; wherefore we know of a surety that the work is true. And we also testify that we have seen the engravings which are upon the plates; and they have been shown unto us by the power of God, and not of man. And we declare with words of soberness, that an angel of God came down from heaven, and he brought and laid before our eyes, that we beheld and saw the plates, and the engravings thereon; and we know that it is by the grace of God the Father, and our Lord Jesus Christ, that we beheld and bear record that these things are true. And it is marvelous in our eyes. Nevertheless, the voice of the Lord commanded us that we should bear record of it; wherefore, to be obedient unto the commandments of God, we bear testimony of these things. And we know that if we are faithful in Christ, we shall rid our garments of the blood of all men, and be found spotless before the judgment-seat of Christ, and shall dwell with him eternally in the heavens. And the honor be to the Father, and to the Son, and to the Holy Ghost, which is one God. Amen.
>
> Oliver Cowdery
> David Whitmer
> Martin Harris

The Eight Witnesses

"We Did Handle with Our Hands"

Soon after the Three Witnesses saw the plates in Fayette, New York, eight witnesses were privileged to heft the plates in Manchester, New York. They retired to the solitude of a wooded area near the Smith family residence. The Prophet Joseph Smith took the plates from a cloth container and laid them before their eyes. Each of the men—from fifty-eight-year-old Joseph Smith, Sr., to Peter Whitmer, Jr., a youth of nineteen years—handled the plates and examined the ancient engravings. They bore testimony of this sacred event, which testimony is contained in the prefatory pages of the Book of Mormon:

> Be it known unto all nations, kindreds, tongues, and people, unto whom this work shall come: That Joseph Smith, Jun., the translator of this work, has shown unto us the plates of which hath been spoken, which have the appearance of gold; and as many of the leaves as the said Smith has translated we did handle with our hands; and we also saw the engravings thereon, all of which has the appearance of ancient work, and of curious workmanship. And this we bear record with words of soberness, that the said Smith has shown unto us, for we have seen and hefted, and know of a surety that the said Smith has got the plates of which we have spoken. And we give our names unto the world, to witness unto the world that which we have seen. And we lie not, God bearing witness of it.

Christian Whitmer	Hiram Page
Jacob Whitmer	Joseph Smith, Sn.
Peter Whitmer, Jun.	Hyrum Smith
John Whitmer	Samuel H. Smith

Katherine Smith Salisbury

"I Have Wept like a Child"

Katherine Salisbury, sister of the Prophet Joseph Smith, wrote that she believed the Book of Mormon to be true. She compared it to 1 Corinthians 12:3, "No man can say that Jesus is the Lord, but by the Holy Ghost." When she first saw the Book of Mormon, she was convinced that "without God's guidance her brother could not have brought forth such a work" (Salisbury 260). Nevertheless, her full conversion occurred as she read the book with a prayerful heart. "I can testify to the fact of the coming forth of the Book of Mormon," she affirmed, "and also to its truth, and the truth of the everlasting gospel as contained therein. . . . Many times when I have read its sacred pages, I have wept like a child, while the Spirit has borne witness with my spirit of its truth." (Salisbury 260.)

Samuel Smith

"The Greatest Work"

Samuel Harrison Smith, brother of the Prophet Joseph Smith and one of the Eight Witnesses of the Book of Mormon, was called to be the first missionary for the Church. At the age of twenty-two, he left Palmyra to journey through neighboring towns and share the newly published scripture. After walking twenty-five miles the first day, Samuel asked an innkeeper for a night's lodging. The innkeeper not only refused Samuel lodging but also ordered him off the premises. The young Elder spent that first night of his mission under an apple tree.

The next day Samuel stopped at the home of Reverend John P. Greene, a Methodist minister in Mendon, New York. Reverend Greene was not interested in reading the Book of Mormon, but indicated that he would accept a copy and keep a subscription list of anyone who might want to purchase the book. Earlier another preacher, Phinehas Young, had purchased a copy and promised Samuel he would read it. Phinehas thought Samuel was deceived and that the book might likewise deceive his own congregation; therefore, as a minister he felt he had the right to expose the deception and save his people from error. Samuel returned from this brief mission to his home in Palmyra feeling that his efforts had been fruitless. He was unaware that these two copies of the Book of Mormon would be the means of converting a neighborhood.

The first to read Reverend Greene's copy was his wife, Rhoda. She read its contents with great interest, then urged her reluctant husband to read it. Both later joined the Church.

Phinehas Young's copy of the Book of Mormon was known to have inspired the curiosity of many neighbors. His father, John Young, read it first and declared to Phinehas that it "was the greatest work, and the clearest from error of any he had ever seen, the Bible not excepted" (Young 52). Fanny Young read it next, and called it a revelation. During the summer the book was passed around among the entire family—all read it, all believed its truth. The same copy was read by Brigham Young, and some two years later in April 1832, after his own careful study and investigation of the Book of Mormon, he and the other members of the family were baptized. Heber C. Kimball read this same copy of the Book of Mormon in his turn and was also baptized in April 1832.

Lucy Mack Smith

"One Third of Your Church"

The Prophet's mother, Lucy Mack Smith, did not hesitate to proclaim the power of the Book of Mormon and her son's role in translating the word of God. She displayed this confidence to Mr. Ruggles, a Presbyterian pastor. According to Mother Smith's account, upon being introduced to her the pastor remarked, "And you are the mother of that poor, foolish, silly boy, Joe Smith, who pretended to translate the Book of Mormon." Lucy firmly replied, "I am, sir, the mother of Joseph Smith; but why do you apply to him such epithets as those?" The reverend returned, "Because that he should imagine he was going to break down all other churches with that simple 'Mormon' book." Lucy's account goes on to show how she defended her son's character and the authenticity of the Book of Mormon:

> "Did you ever read that book?" I inquired.
> "No," said he, "it is beneath my notice."
> "But," rejoined I, "the Scriptures say, 'prove all things'; and, now, sir, let me tell you boldly, that that book contains the everlasting gospel, and it was written for the salvation of your soul, by the gift and power of the Holy Ghost."
> "Pooh," said the minister, "nonsense—I am not afraid of any member of my church being led astray by such stuff; they have too much intelligence."

"Now, Mr. Ruggles," said I, and spoke with emphasis, for the Spirit of God was upon me, "mark my words—as true as God lives, before three years we will have more than one-third of your church; and, sir, whether you believe it or not, we will take the very deacon, too." (*History of Joseph Smith* 215–16.)

The minister responded to Lucy's vow with a hearty laugh, but she remained undaunted and during the next four weeks "labored incessantly for the truth's sake." Soon afterwards, Elder Jared Carter was called to preach in that vicinity. Lucy wrote, "He went immediately into the midst of Mr. Ruggles' church, and, in a short time, brought away seventy of his best members, among whom was the deacon [Samuel Bent], just as I told the minister." (*History of Joseph Smith* 216-17.)

Simeon Doget Carter

"It Wrought Deeply upon His Mind"

Missionary Parley P. Pratt was invited into the home of Simeon Carter in 1830. Parley was treated with kindness by Simeon, and together they read from the Book of Mormon. However, a local officer of the court soon entered the Carter home with a warrant for Parley's arrest on what Parley termed "a very frivolous charge" (36). As Parley went with the officer to stand trial before a judge, he left a copy of the Book of Mormon with Simeon. In his autobiography, Parley wrote about the power and influence that single book had upon Simeon and his neighborhood:

> The Book of Mormon, which I dropped at the house of Simeon Carter, when taken by the officer, was by these circumstances left with him. He read it with attention. It wrought deeply upon his mind, and he went fifty miles to the church we had left in Kirtland, and was there baptized and ordained an Elder. He then returned to his home and commenced to preach and baptize. A church of about sixty members was soon organized in the place. (39.)

John Murdock

"Filled with the Spirit"

For many years, John Murdock had diligently prayed to the Lord to "not only know the truth but to also find a people that lived according to truth." In 1830, Oliver Cowdery, Parley P. Pratt, Peter Whitmer, and Ziba Peterson shared the truths of the Book of Mormon with him. John was soon convinced that these Mormon Elders had not only truth but also the "authority to administer the ordinances of the Gospel." (Murdock, Journal.) He was baptized on 5 November 1830 by Elder Pratt.

John then returned to his family after a four-day absence, carrying a copy of the Book of Mormon to read to them. He recorded: "They believed it for I was filled with the spirit when I read." Soon after, the Spirit was so strong that John was able to baptize his family and commence preaching from the Book of Mormon. He wrote:

> Through my preaching in about 4 months about seventy Souls were aded [*sic*] to the Church & being thronged with inquirers I quit other business & left my own house & moved my family in with Bro C. [Caleb] Baldwin & gave my full time to the ministry. (Murdock, Journal.)

Zina Diantha Huntington Young

"Truth, Truth, Truth!"

When Zina Young was interviewed by a reporter from the *Young Woman's Journal,* she was told, "Our Mutual girls would enjoy a glimpse into the inner lives of . . . [the] noble ones" (Talmage 255). Zina responded by sharing with the reporter an experience she had when she was thirteen years old and lived in Watertown, New York, about sixty miles from the Hill Cumorah. At that time there were malicious rumors circulating in her neighborhood about the coming forth of the Book of Mormon. In spite of these falsehoods, Zina's parents were soon converted to the Church. Other converts began to visit their home, including Hyrum Smith and David Whitmer, who brought a copy of the first edition of the Book of Mormon. She told of her first encounter with this glorious book:

When I entered the room and read the title of the book that was lying on the window sill, my whole soul was filled with joy. Without opening it I clasped it to my heart and exclaimed, "O Truth, Truth, Truth!" I knew it had been brought forth by an angel's hand and the feeling that possessed me was one of supreme ecstasy. From that moment until the present I have never had a doubt of its divinity. (Qtd. in Talmage 256.)

After describing her reaction at seeing the Book of Mormon, Zina showed the reporter the copy of that book "which long years before had brought such unspeakable joy to her heart" (Talmage 257).

William Miller

"Scarcely Resting to Eat"

William Miller's parents were known in rural New York society for their prominence and wealth, as well as their divergent religious views. Although Father Miller was known by his contemporaries as "strictly moral and honest in his dealings with his fellow-men," he had not joined any religious sect. Mother Miller was a practicing Presbyterian, and although her husband would not accompany her to church meetings, he did not hinder her attendance. This religious disparity continued until 1831, when their son William was seventeen years old. At this time "a religious wave passed over their part of the country, and all were anxious to experience its influence—experience of change of heart." (Jenson 1:481.) Young William was no exception.

He attended the revivals, and after repeated solicitations had his name put down on six months' trial—it being the rule to take persons on a short trial to prove their sincerity, before admitting them to membership. Just after taking this step he heard an Elder preach the new and strange doctrines then advocated by the "Mormons," which set him to read the Scriptures, to ascertain for himself as to the truth. He also obtained a Book of Mormon and carefully read its contents, scarcely resting to eat and drink, and found it consistent with the Bible. He attended all the Latter-day Saint meetings in the vicinity for a year, which resulted in his ultimately joining the Latter-day Saints. (Jenson 1:481.)

Morris Charles Phelps

"I Could Not Refrain from Weeping"

In 1831 Morris Phelps received a letter from a relative, informing him of a new church in Ohio. She wrote that this church was based on a book entitled the Book of Mormon, which had been translated from writings on gold plates "found by the direction of an angel in York State" (Morris Phelps, Autobiography). She further indicated that many families who believed in the Book of Mormon were living together on Isaac Morley's farm, including the Edward Partridge family. Morris had been acquainted with the Morleys and Partridges since his boyhood and had the utmost respect for both families. In her letter, this relative encouraged Morris to treat kindly any preachers from the new church who might appear in his vicinity.

Morris wrote that the news contained in this letter "created such a curiosity and anxiety mingled with joy that I could not refrain from weeping" (Autobiography).

The next day he shared his thoughts with his neighbor, Charles C. Rich. Like Morris, Charles was desirous to learn more of the Book of Mormon and the latter-day prophet. Morris's autobiography describes his neighbor's conversion:

> Several years after he spoke of a peculiar sensation of feeling that penetrated his whole sistem [sic] that made his spirit buoiant [sic] and full of joy but he knew not what it meant. But now said he: I know that it was the spirit of God testifying to me of the truth of the Prophet and Book of Mormon.

Morris also read the letter to Mr. Porter, who was anxious to learn more. As news of the Book of Mormon began to spread from one friend to another and curiosity increased, Morris determined to write to Isaac Morley and Edward Partridge "for further information of the Book and Prophet" (Autobiography). His intense fascination with the new book of scripture led to his reading of the book and his subsequent baptism into the Church.

Noah Packard

"The Scriptures Were Opened to Our Understanding"

In 1831 a rumor had circulated in Ohio that a gold Bible had been dug out of the earth. When Noah Packard heard local preachers denounce it, he believed that false prophets and teachers desired to deceive the very elect. His opinion changed when William Jolly and his family became near neighbors. They believed in the gold Bible, and Mrs. Jolly presented a copy to Noah, asking him to read it. He wrote of his initial reaction to his neighbor's request and of his embracing of its truth:

> I told her I would, and took it and carried it home and placing the book against my forehead asked secretly the Lord if that work was His, He would make it manifest to me. I then opened the book and commenced reading aloud that my wife might also hear it. We read it through and I commenced reading it the second time and the Lord poured out His spirit upon me and the scriptures were opened to our understanding, and we were convinced that the Book of Mormon was a true record of the Aborigines of America containing the fulness of the gospel of Jesus Christ which was to come forth at the time of the restitution of the House of Israel.
>
> Accordingly I and my wife were baptized in the town of Parkman [Ohio] by Parley P. Pratt and were confirmed in the Church of Jesus Christ of Latter-day Saints, under his hands and Hyrum Smith's hands, the day I am unable to state, but think it was between the first and fifth of June 1832. (Packard, Autobiography.)

George Cannon

"Unless It Were True"

Elder John Taylor, a newly ordained member of the Council of the Twelve Apostles, left for England in 1839 carrying a letter from his wife to her brother, George Cannon. This letter introduced John and opened to him the doors of the Cannon home in Liverpool.

After John's initial visit, Mother Cannon said to her young son, George Q. Cannon, "George, there goes a man of God. He is come to bring salvation to your father's house." (Evans and Cannon 34.) On John's second meeting with the family, they sang the hymns of Zion, and he left them with a copy of the Book of Mormon. George Cannon read the Book of Mormon through twice before remarking, "No wicked man could write such a book as this; and no good man would write it, unless it were true and he were commanded of God to do so" (Evans and Cannon 35). The Cannon family was baptized and soon migrated to Nauvoo, Illinois, to join the Saints of God.

Daniel Tyler

"I Believed Every Word"

At the conclusion of a meeting held in the home of Joseph Hartshorn, fifteen-year-old Daniel Tyler opened a copy of the Book of Mormon that had been lying on the table. He began to read in the preface (the substance of which is now contained in Doctrine and Covenants 10) regarding the loss of the 116-page manuscript. Suddenly, his eighteen-year-old brother, William, grabbed the book out of his hands and closed it, exclaiming that "good people said it carried with it a spirit of witchcraft, which caused those who read it to be bewitched and join the 'Mormon' church" (Tyler 24).

Daniel was surprised at this outburst because it seemed so contrary to his brother's character. However, Daniel soon became concerned that William might be right, for, as he later wrote, "the last words I read were so riveted upon my mind that I sometimes feared there was some truth in the remark about the book being bewitching." The last words he had read, which were part of the preface, were, "I will show unto them that my wisdom is greater than the cunning of the devil" (see D&C 10:43). Daniel later related:

> Before leaving the place the Elders baptized three persons. My father soon became a bitter enemy. I believed

every word of the first discourse referred to previously, but dared not make my belief known because of my youth and the bitterness of my father. He admitted that the "Mormon" doctrines were true, but claimed that the members of that church had adopted them to cover up a fraud. All classes of people joined in the cry, "Beware of false prophets who come to you in sheep's clothing," etc., telling ridiculous stories about "Old Joe Smith walking on the water," pretended miracles, angels being caught, etc. (24.)

Amid this ridicule, Daniel clung to his early views of the Book of Mormon and soon accepted baptism into The Church of Jesus Christ of Latter-day Saints.

Harrison Burgess

"A Testimony of These Things"

In July 1832, Harrison Burgess's initial response to hearing the gospel fulness was to proclaim his conviction that the Book of Mormon was the word of God. Accordingly, he was baptized and was soon invited to speak before a Church congregation. In his speech he firmly declared the truthfulness of the Book of Mormon. However, as he later wrote, on the following day "something seemed to whisper to me, 'Do you know the Book of Mormon is true?' " His mind became perplexed, darkened, and tormented. He was so distraught that he retired to the woods to seek for divine guidance. He wrote of this experience:

The misery and distress that I there experienced cannot be described. The tempter all the while seemed to say, "Do you know the Book of Mormon is true?" I remained in this situation about two hours. Finally I resolved to know, by exercising faith similar to that which the brother of Jared possessed, whether I had proclaimed the truth or not,and commenced praying to the God of heaven for a testimony of these things. Suddenly a glorious personage clothed in white stood before me and exhibited to my view the plates from which the Book of Mormon was taken. (Burgess 65-66.)

3

Testimonies of the
Book of Mormon

A few of the early Saints wrote details of their conversion to The Church of Jesus Christ of Latter-day Saints through the Book of Mormon. Journals and family stories reveal the depth of their conviction, sacrifice, and willingness to be numbered among the believers. Their stories depict knowing by the Spirit of the coming forth of the Book of Mormon, gaining a testimony of the book, and defending that holy scripture. These stories are filled with restless searching, as the disciple begins his or her quest for new religious truth. The accounts end with a quiet, abiding faith in God and an assurance that their quest has been realized in the Book of Mormon.

Benjamin Brown

Benjamin Brown, son of Asa Brown and Sarah Moon, was born on 30 September 1794 in Queensbury, Washington, New York. He married Sarah Mumford on 12 September 1819, and they became the parents of five children. In 1835 Benjamin was baptized into the Church in New York, and soon removed to Kirtland, Ohio, where he attended the dedication of the Kirtland Temple. Religious persecution forced him to flee to Missouri, to Illinois, and finally to the Salt Lake Valley. There he served as bishop of the Salt Lake City Fourth Ward. He was a proselyting missionary to the eastern states, Canada, and Great Britain. Benjamin died on 22 May 1878 in Salt Lake City at the age of eighty-three.

In his autobiography, Benjamin recalled his initial prejudice against the Book of Mormon. He described a dark feeling that permeated his mind until he resolved to read the Bible. This reading, coupled with a powerful impression to read the Book of Mormon and a subsequent visitation from heavenly messengers, led to his conversion.

❀   ❀   ❀

A few days after, curiosity led me to visit the Latter-day Saints, amongst whom I witnessed a fulfillment of the prediction, for I beheld a manifestation of the gifts of prophecy and tongues, and received the latter myself.

Notwithstanding that the above confirmation which I received of the truth of the Church of the Latter-day Saints, was very great, I did not feel sufficiently convinced to be induced to join them at once. I had experienced the Spirit of the Lord in a similar way elsewhere, so that when the elders of the Church, at this meeting, urged upon me to yield obedience to the gospel they preached, which possessed such evidences as the manifestation of the ancient gifts, I treated the elders very lightly, and replied, that as for the gift of tongues, I could speak in tongues as well as any of them. So I could, for directly one of them manifested this gift, the gift of tongues rested upon me, and gave me the same power. Thus did the devil seek to blind me, and turn that testimony which the Lord had given me for the truth, almost into an evidence against it! However, I procured a Book of Mormon, and took it home to read, determined to investigate until I was fully satisfied. But I had scarcely begun to read, before I felt greatly to dislike the book. Ere I had perused ten pages, I rejected it altogether. . . .

But, oh! the darkness that seized me as soon as I had made this resolution! The light that was in me became darkness, and how great it was, no language can describe. All knowledge of religious truth seemed to forsake me, and if I attempted to quote scripture, my recollection failed, after the first word or so! So remarkable was this, that it excited reflection, and caused me to marvel, and finally I determined to repent of my resolve respecting the Bible, and I commenced to read again. The book was hardly in my hand, when, as in a moment, my light and recollection returned as usual. This made me rejoice, and immediately the idea flashed across my mind, "What have you done with the Book of Mormon? Behave as fairly to that." I soon reprocured it. But, even this time, I felt prejudiced against the book. I resolved, however, to read it through, and I persevered in its perusal, till I came to that part where Jesus, on visiting the continent of America, after his resurrection, grants the request of three of the twelve whom he had chosen, to permit them to live until His Second Coming on the earth (like unto John spoken of in the Bible).

Here my mind half yielded to the belief which arose within me, that perhaps it might be true, whereupon I took the book and laid it before the Lord, and pleaded with him in prayer for a testimony whether it was true or false, and, as I found it stated that the three Nephites had power to show themselves to any persons they might wish to, Jews or Gentiles, I asked the Lord to allow me to see them for a witness and testimony of the truth of the Book of Mormon, and I covenanted with him, if he complied with my request, that I would preach it even at the expense of my life, should it be necessary.

The Lord heard my prayer, and, about five days after, two of the three visited me in my bedroom. I did not see them come, but I found them there. One spoke to me for some time, and reproved me sharply on account of my behavior at the time when I first attended the meeting of the Saints, and treated so lightly the gift of tongues. He told me never, as long as I lived, to do so again, for I had grieved the Spirit of the Lord, by whose power that gift had been given. This personage spoke in the Nephite language, but I understood, by the Spirit which accompanied him, every word as plainly as if he had spoken in English. I recognized the language to be the same as that in which I had heard Father Fisher speak at the meeting. Such a rebuke, with such power, I never had in my life before or since, and never wish to have again. I was dumb before my rebuker, for I knew that what he said was right, and I felt deserving of it.

How these men went, I do not know, but directly they were gone, the Spirit of the Lord said to me, "Now, you know for yourself! You have seen and heard! If you now fall away, there is no forgiveness for you." Did I not know then, that the Book of Mormon was true, and that Joseph Smith was a Prophet of the

Lord? Surely I did, and I do now, as surely as I know that I live. (From Brown, *Testimonies for the Truth* 5.)

Jared Carter

Jared Carter, son of Gideon Carter and Johannah Sims, was born on 14 January 1801 in Benson, Rutland, Vermont. He married Lydia Ames on 20 September 1825, and they became the parents of nine children. On 20 February 1831, after reading and praying about the Book of Mormon, Jared was baptized by Hyrum Smith. Soon after his conversion, he had "no mind to pursue [his] business" (Carter, Journal), having acquired an ardent desire to preach the truths he had discovered in the Book of Mormon. Jared labored as a missionary in New York, Vermont, Ohio, Pennsylvania, Michigan, Massachusetts, Missouri, and Connecticut. He served in the Kirtland and Far West high councils before being disfellowshipped on 8 September 1844.

Jared wrote an account of his early days in the Church, as he explained, "for I do not make a journal of which took place before I heard of the Church of Christ" (Carter, Journal). This account describes his first reading of the Book of Mormon and his conversion to the Church.

❋　❋　❋

It was at this time that I heard of the Book of Mormon as I was going on business to be gone for several weeks. I had not got more than twelve miles from home before I, for the first time, heard of the Book of Mormon at the house of Mr. Peeks [John Peck], who lived in the town of Lile[?], which not withstanding, he himself was opposed to the work. This caused much astonishment to fill my mind and after reading awhile in the Book of Mormon and praying earnestly to the Lord that he would show me the truth of the book, I became immediately convinced that it was a revelation of God and it had such an influence on my mind that I had no mind to pursue my business. Notwithstanding, I had, just before, a mind to go a considerable journey to be gone for some weeks. But I found I was completely unqualified for any business until I should go and assist the Church of Christ. I therefore returned home.

I told my companion what I had heard and seen. I told her

that [torn] that I should go and see the people [torn]. My companion did not think as I did concerning the thing of which I had been relating to her but she told me that she thought it was delusion and was unwilling that I should go to visit the people. But I concluded that I should go to see them as soon that my companion would be willing that I should go and it seemed to me "requisite" that she should be willing.

I continued praying earnestly that I might know the will of my God to do my duty. I, at length, became convinced that it was my duty to go and see the Church of Christ. I told my companion my feelings. She answered me that she was entirely willing that I should go. Accordingly, I went from Chenango, a town in Broome County, state of New York, where we lived, to the town of Coalsville. On the way to this place I made some inquiry of the people that I met with of this people who believed in the Book of Mormon, which they had. And I heard all manner of statements concerning them almost excepting there was no good said of them and I found that the most wicked and profane were the most ready to rail against them. On seeing this, I, instead of being convinced that there was no truth in the work, . . . I became more and more convinced in the belief of this work, that it was the work spoken of in the prophecies that should take place in the last days, even the great gathering of Israel the second time.

I observed that as I believed in the work that I received the manifestations of the spirit of God. My mind was joyfully entertained in view of the prophecies and of this most glorious work of the Lord. On visiting the Church of Christ, at Coalsville and having an interview with them, I felt it my duty to separate from Babylon and be baptized. Accordingly I was baptized by Hyrum Smith about the 20th of February, for the remission of sins & as I was baptized I felt the influences of the Spirit of God for as I stepped out of the water I was wrapped in the spirit both soul & body even so that the chill of the cold water was taken from me. (From Carter, Journal.)

Solomon Chamberlain

Solomon Chamberlain, son of Joel Chamberlain and Sarah Dean, was born on 30 July 1788 in Old Canaan, Litchfield, Connecticut. He married Hope Haskin on 23 October 1809 in Pownal,

Vermont, and they became the parents of three children. Solomon was baptized by Joseph Smith in April 1830 and was soon ordained a teacher in the Aaronic Priesthood. He was driven with the Saints from Ohio to Missouri, and from Missouri to Illinois. On 17 June 1845 he received his patriarchal blessing, and on 18 December 1845 he was given his endowment in the Nauvoo Temple. He joined exiled Saints in the westward trek to the Salt Lake Valley. Solomon died on 20 March 1863 in Washington, Washington, Utah, at the age of seventy-four.

In his autobiography Solomon explained that after his father died when Solomon was around age eight, for about ten years Solomon "lived a very wicked life" until he had "a vision of hell." This vision so alarmed him that he changed his life-style and began to earnestly search for revealed truth. His words describe his youth, his search, and his joy in finding the Book of Mormon.

✳   ✳   ✳

My father was an honest, hard-working man, a farmer by trade, and earned his bread by the sweat of his brow, and accumulated considerable property, and died when I was about 8 years old, and my mother died about 10 years after. What little property I received from my father's estate did me little or no good, and I began the world like my father, earned my bread by the sweat of my face. I soon learned the cooper's trade and worked the most of my days at that. From the time my father died, till I was 19 years of age I lived a very wicked life. About that time, I had a vision of hell, and which alarmed me very much, and I reformed and had another of three heavens, and their glories, and the third one, far exceeded the others. My visions so alarmed me, I was in sorrow and repentance for many days, on account of my sins, I thought I would give all the world if I could find a man, that could tell me what I should do to be saved. I sought much, but could find none. I thought I would go to the Presbyterian Minister and enquire of him, I accordingly went, and asked him what I should do to be saved, he appeared like a man astonished, he said I must wait the Lord's due time, and in His own due time he would bring me in: as all others had failed I thought I would go to God and plead for mercy, and if I went to hell, I would go praying, and I cried unto the Lord night and day, for the forgiveness of my sins. Like Enos of old, till at length the Lord said, Solomon, thy sins are forgiven thee,

go in peace and sin no more. My heart then leaped for joy unspeakable, I now joined the Methodist Order, and thought they
were the rightest of any on the earth.

About the year 1814 or 1815, the Reformed Methodists
broke off from the Episcopal Methodists. I was in hope that
they were right. [This last sentence was crossed out in the original manuscript.] I found them to be more right than the Episcopal, and joined them. About this time the Lord showed me in
a vision, that there was no people on the earth that was right,
and that faith was gone from the earth, excepting a few and
that all churches were corrupt. I further saw in vision, that he
would soon raise up a church, that would be after the Apostolic
Order, that there would be in it the same powers, and gifts that
were in the days of Christ, and that I should live to see the day,
and that there would a book come forth, like unto the Bible and
the people would [be] guided by it, as well as the Bible. This was
in the year of 1816. I then believed in gifts and miracles as the
Latter-day Saints do, for which I was much persecuted and
called deluded. This vision I received from an Angel or Spirit
from the Eternal world that told me these things.

About the time that Joseph Smith found the gold record, I
began to feel that the time was drawing near, that the Lord
would in some shape or other, bring forth his church. I made
some inquiry through the country where I traveled if there was
any strange work of God, such as had not been on the earth
since the days of Christ. I could hear of none. I was living about
20 miles east of where the gold record was found, on the Erie
Canal. I had occasion to go on a visit into Upper Canada. I took
boat for Lockport, when the boat came to Palmyra, I felt as if
some Genie or good Spirit told me to leave the boat. This was a
few miles from where the record was found. After leaving the
boat, the spirit manifested to me, to travel a South course. I did
so for about 3 miles. I had not yet heard of the Gold Bible (so
called) [Book of Mormon] nor any of the [Joseph] Smith family. I
was a stranger in that part of the country, a town where I never
before had set my foot, and knew no one in the town. It was
now about sundown, and my guide directed me to put up for
the night, which I did to a farm house. In the morning, the
people of the house asked me if I had heard of the Gold Bible
[Book of Mormon]. When they said Gold Bible, there was a
power like electricity went from the top of my head to the end of
my toes. This was the first time I ever heard of the Gold Bible. I

was now within half a mile of the Smith family where Joseph lived. From the time I left the boat until now, I was wholly led by the Spirit or my Genie. The women spoke considerable of the Gold Bible that Joseph Smith had found. When she mentioned Gold Bible, I felt a shock of the power of God go from head to foot. I said to myself, I shall soon find why I have been led in this singular manner. I soon made my way across lots, to Father Smith's and found Hyrum walking the floor. As I entered the door, I said, peace be to this house. He looked at me as one astonished, and said, I hope it will be peace. I then said, is there anyone here that believes in visions or revelations. He said, yes, we are a visionary house. I said, then I will give you one of my pamphlets, which was visionary, and of my own experience. They then called the people together, which consisted of five or six men who were out at the door. Father Smith was one and some of the Whitmer's. They then sat down and read my pamphlet. Hyrum read first, but was so affected he could not read it. He then gave it to a man, which I learned was Christian Whitmer, he finished reading it. I then opened my mouth and began to preach to them, in the words that the angel had made known to me in the vision, that all Churches and Denominations on the earth had become corrupt, and no church of God on the earth, but that he would shortly raise up a church that would never be confounded nor brought down and be like unto the Apostolic Church. They wondered greatly who had been telling me these things, for said they we have the same things wrote down in our house, taken from the Gold record, that you are preaching to us. I said, the Lord told me these things a number of years ago. I then said, if you are a visionary house, I wish you would make known some of your discoveries, for I think I can bear them. They then made known to me that they had obtained a gold record, and just finished translating it here. Now, the Lord revealed to me by the gift and power of the Holy Ghost that this was the work I had been looking for. Here I stayed 2 days and they instructed me, in the manuscripts of the Book of Mormon. After I had been here two days, I went with Hyrum and some others to Palmyra printing office where they began to print the Book of Mormon, and as soon as they had printed 64 pages, I took them with their leave and pursued my journey to Canada, and I preached all that I knew concerning Mormonism, to all both high and low, rich and poor, and thus you see this was the first that ever printed

Mormonism was preached to this generation. I did not see anyone in traveling for 7 or 800 miles, that had ever heard of the Gold Bible (so called). I exhorted all people to prepare for the great work of God that was now about to come forth, and it would never be brought down nor confounded. As soon as the book was printed, I took 8 or 10 of them and traveled for 8 days, and sold one in that time. About this time I thought if I could see the Reformed Methodists I could convince them of the truth of the Book of Mormon. I accordingly went to one of their conferences, where I met about 40 of their preachers and labored with them for two days to convince them of the truth of the Book of Mormon, and they utterly rejected me and the Book of Mormon. One of their greatest preachers so called, by the name of Buckly, (if I mistake not) abused me very bad, and ordered me off from their premises. He was soon taken crazy, and died a miserable death. At this conference was Brigham and his brother Phine[h]as Young. They did not oppose me but used me well. On my way home I stopped at their camp meeting, where I found one of their greatest preachers, whom I contended with concerning the Book of Mormon, by the name of William Lake, who utterly condemned it and rejected it, who spurned at me and the Book and said, if it was of God, do you think He would send such a little upstart as you are around with it? But he soon after died a poor drunken sot. While on my way home I stopped at a Free Will Baptist Church, and preached to a large congregation, and they received the work, but there was no one to baptize them. The Church was not yet organized, but was soon after, April 6th, 1830. A few days after, I was baptized in the waters of Seneca Lake, by Joseph Smith. (From Chamberlain, Autobiography.)

Rachel Ridgway Ivins Grant

Rachel Ridgway Ivins, daughter of Caleb Ivins, Jr., and Edith Ridgway, was born on 7 March 1821 in Hornerstown, Monmouth, New Jersey. Her father died when she was six years old, and her mother died when she was nine. As a young woman she began to search for a religion that could make her happy. In 1840, Rachel listened to Mormon Elders and accepted their challenge of baptism. She joined the Saints in Nauvoo, Illinois, where

Rachel Ridgway Ivins Grant

on 15 October 1843 she was given her patriarchal blessing. She married Jedediah Morgan Grant on 29 November 1855 in Salt Lake City, and they became the parents of one son, Heber J. Grant. For thirty-five years she served as president of the Relief Society in the Salt Lake City Thirteenth Ward. Rachel died on 27 January 1909 in Salt Lake City at the age of eighty-eight.

Rachel wrote an account of her earliest history, including the incidents that led to her conversion and her fervent testimony of the gospel. Her conversion story begins with the influence of her grandparents' "silent worship," and ends with the happiness she found within the restored gospel of Jesus Christ.

❋   ❋   ❋

My grandparents on both sides were Quakers, consequently I was brought up under that influence. But the silent worship of the Friends did not satisfy the cravings of my soul. I longed to hear the beautiful hymns that my mother taught to her little children even in our tender years, and the spirit often moved me to burst out in songs of praise, and it was with difficulty that I could refrain from doing so.

At the age of sixteen years with the consent of my relatives,

I joined the Baptist Church. The singing pleased me and the prayers were somewhat inspiring, but the sermons were not much more satisfactory than the none-at-all of the Quakers. I was religiously inclined but not of the long-faced variety. I thought religion ought to make people happier and that was the kind of religion I was looking for.

About this time we heard of some strange preachers called "Mormons" who had come to our neighborhood. I concluded they were some of the false prophets that the Bible speaks of and I had no desire to see or hear them. . . .

I went to the meeting on Saturday but when she [her sister, Anna] asked me to go on Sunday I did not know whether I ought to break the Sabbath day by going to hear them or not. But I finally went. Upon returning home I went to my room, knelt down and asked the Lord to forgive me for thus breaking the Sabbath day.

I attended some more meetings and commenced reading the "Book of Mormon," "Voice of Warning" and other works, and was soon convinced that they were true. A new light seemed to break upon me. The scriptures were plainer to my mind, and the light of the everlasting gospel began to illumine my soul. While thus investigating, a little child died whose mother had joined the Latter-day Saints. The Baptist minister took occasion to refer to the death of the little one, regretting that its parents had neglected to have it baptized, and that thereby it was lost and could not have salvation. I afterwards heard Elder Orson Hyde preach the funeral sermon. He portrayed the glories of our Father's kingdom and the saved condition of the little innocent ones who died before they came to [the] years of accountability—"For of such is the Kingdom of Heaven."

The contrast was very great, showing one to be false and the other true. I was steadily being drawn to the gospel net.

One day while attending the Baptist prayer meeting our pastor admonished me for the course I was taking and said if I did not stop going to the Mormon meetings I could not hold my seat in the Baptist Church, and they would be obliged to disfellowship me for listening to false doctrines.

This seemed to settle the question with me. One wanted to hold me against my convictions, and the other was free salvation, without money and without price.

I soon handed in my name for baptism and rendered willing obedience to the first four requirements of the gospel of Jesus Christ as revealed through the Prophet Joseph in the last dispensation of the fulness of times. And oh, what joy filled my being! I could sing all the day long and rejoice in the glorious promises of the gospel. (Qtd. in Judd 228-29.)

Jacob Hamblin

Jacob Hamblin, son of Isaiah Hamblin and Daphne Haynes, was born on 2 April 1819 in Ashtabula County, Ohio. He married Lucinda Taylor on 30 April 1839, and they became the parents of four children. As a young man, he believed in the teachings of the Bible but doubted that he would find a true religion. Then, at the age of twenty-two, he heard of the Book of Mormon. After reading this sacred text, he was baptized on 3 March 1842 by Lyman Stoddard.

Jacob soon moved to Nauvoo, Illinois, to be with other Latter-day Saints. Persecution forced him to join the western exodus to the Great Salt Lake Valley. In the valley his friendship with the Indians began with a heavenly inspiration: "It was . . . made manifest to me that if I would not thirst for their [the Indians'] blood, I should never fall by their hands" (Little 223). He was or-dained an "apostle to the Lamanites" by Brigham Young. Jacob died on 31 August 1886 in Pleasanton, Socorro, New Mexico, at the age of sixty-seven.

Jacob told of his first reaction to reading the Book of Mormon and of his hesitancy to join the persecuted Mormons. His wife and children rejected his new-found belief, yet his personal sac-rifice was sustained by a heavenly manifestation.

✳   ✳   ✳

In February, 1842, a neighbor called at my house and told me that he had heard a "Mormon" Elder preach. He asserted that he preached more Bible doctrine than any other man he had ever listened to, and that he knew what he preached was true. He claimed that the gospel had been restored to the earth, and that it was the privilege of all who heard it to know and un-derstand it for themselves.

What this neighbor told me so influenced my mind, that I could scarcely attend to my ordinary business.

The Elder had left an appointment to preach again at the same place, and I went to hear him. When I entered the house he had already commenced his discourse. I shall never forget

Jacob Hamblin

the feeling that came over me when I saw his face and heard his voice. He preached that which I had long been seeking for; I felt that it was indeed the gospel.

The principles he taught appeared so plain and natural, that I thought it would be easy to convince any one of their truth. In closing his remarks, the Elder bore testimony to the truth of the gospel.

The query came to my mind: "How shall I know whether or not these things are so, and be satisfied? As if the Spirit prompted him to answer my inquiry, he again arose to his feet and said: "If there is anyone in the congregation who wishes to know how he can satisfy himself of the truth of these things, I can assure him that if he will be baptized, and have hands laid upon him for the gift of the Holy Ghost, he shall have an assurance of their truth."

This so fired up my mind, that I at once determined to be baptized, and that too, if necessary, at the sacrifice of the friendship of my kindred and of every earthly tie.

I immediately went home and informed my wife of my intentions.

She told me that if I was baptized into the "Mormon" Church, I need not expect her to live with me any more.

The evening after the Elder had preached I went in search of him, and found him quite late at night. I told him my purpose, and requested him to give me a "Mormon Bible." He handed me the Old and New Testament.

I said, "I thought you had a new Bible." He then explained about the coming forth of the Book of Mormon, and handed me a copy of it.

The impressions I received at the time cannot be forgotten. The spirit rested upon me and bore testimony of its truth, and I felt like opening my mouth and declaring it to be a revelation from God.

On the 3rd of March, 1842, as soon as it was light in the morning, I started for a pool of water where I had arranged to meet with the Elder, to attend to the ordinance of baptism. On the way, the thought of the sacrifice I was making of wife, of father, mother, brothers, sister and numerous other connections, caused my resolution to waver.

As my pace slackened, some person appeared to come from above, who, I thought, was my grandfather. He seemed to say to me, "Go on, my son; your heart cannot conceive, neither has it entered into your mind to imagine the blessings that are in store for you, if you go on and continue in this work."

I lagged no more, but hurried to the pool, where I was baptized by Elder Lyman Stoddard.

It was said in my confirmation, that the spirits in prison greatly rejoiced over what I had done. I told Elder Stoddard my experience on my way to the water.

He then explained to me the work there was for me to do for my fathers, if I was faithful, all of which I believed and greatly rejoiced in.

On my way home, I called at the house of one of my neighbors. The family asked me if I had not been baptized by the "Mormon" Elder. I replied that I had. They stated that they believed what he preached to be the truth, and hoped they might have the opportunity of being baptized.

The following day Elder Stoddard came to my house, and told me that he had intended to leave the country, but could not go without coming to see me. For what purpose he had come, he knew not.

I related to him what my neighbors had said. He held more

meetings in the place, and organized a branch before leaving. (From Little 203-5.)

Orson Hyde

Orson Hyde, son of Nathan Hyde and Sarah Thorpe, was born on 8 January 1805 in Oxford, New Haven, Connecticut. On 31 October 1830 he was baptized by Sidney Rigdon and one year later was ordained a high priest. Orson married Nancy Marinda Johnson on 4 September 1834 in Geauga County, Ohio, and they became the parents of eleven children. In 1837 he fulfilled a mission to England, and in 1840 he dedicated Jerusalem for the gathering of the Jews. From 1835 to 1878 he served as a member of the Council of the Twelve Apostles, presiding over that body for over twenty-seven years. Orson died on 28 November 1878 in Spring City, Sanpete, Utah, at the age of seventy-three.

During the fall of 1830, Oliver Cowdery, Parley P. Pratt, Ziba Peterson, and Peter Whitmer, Jr., journeyed through Ohio, preaching from the Book of Mormon. Their teaching so intrigued Orson that he began the fervent study of the book that led to his baptism. He recounted his first experience with the Book of Mormon in his autobiography.

* * *

I encountered them [the missionaries]; but perceiving that they were mostly illiterate men, and at the same time observing some examples of superior wisdom and truth in their teaching, I resolved to read the famed 'golden bible,' as it was called.

Accordingly, I procured the book and read a portion of it, but came to the conclusion that it was all a fiction. I preached several times against the 'Mormon' doctrine or rather against the 'Mormon' bible. On one occasion, the people of Ridgeville, near Elyria, sent for me to preach against the 'Mormon' bible. I complied with the request and preached against it. The people congratulated me much, thinking that 'Mormonism' was completely floored. But I, for the first time, thought that the 'Mormon' bible might be the truth of heaven; and fully resolved before leaving the house, that I would never preach against it anymore until I knew more about it, being pretty strongly convicted in my own mind that I was doing wrong. I closed up my school and my preaching in that section, and resolved to go to Kirtland on a visit to my old friends. Elder S. Rigdon, Gilbert and Whitney, and many others of my former friends had embraced the

Orson Hyde

'Mormon' faith. I ventured to tell a few of my confidential friends in Florence my real object in visiting Kirtland. The Prophet, Joseph Smith, Jun., had moved to that place. My object was to get away from the prejudices of the people, and to place myself in a position where I could examine the subject without embarrassment.

Accordingly, in the summer of 1831, I went to Kirtland, and under cover of clerkship in the old store of Whitney and Gilbert, I examined 'Mormonism.' Read the 'Mormon' bible carefully through, attended meetings of the 'Mormons' and others, heard the arguments *pro and con.*, but was careful to say nothing. I prayed much unto the Lord for light and knowledge, for wisdom and spirit to guide me in my examinations and investigations. Often heard the Prophet talk in public and in private upon the subject of the new religion; also heard what the opposition had to say. Listened also to many foolish tales about the Prophet— too foolish to have a place in this narrative. I marked carefully the spirit that attended the opposition, and also the spirit that attended the 'Mormons' and their friends; and after about three months of careful and prayerful investigation, reflection and meditation, I came to the conclusion that the 'Mormons' had more light and a better spirit than their opponents. I concluded that I could not be the loser by joining the 'Mormons,' and as an honest man, conscientiously bound to walk in the best and clearest light I saw, I resolved to be baptized into the new religion. Hence, I attended the Saints' meeting in Kirtland, Sunday, October 30, 1831, and offered myself a candidate for baptism, which was administered to me by the hands of Elder Sidney Rigdon. . . . Not until about three days after did I receive any internal evidence of the special approbation of Heaven of the course I had taken. When one evening behind the counter, the Spirit of the Lord came upon me in so powerful a manner, that I felt like waiting upon no one, and withdrew in private to enjoy the feast alone. This, to me, was a precious season, long to be remembered. (From Hyde 75-76.)

Vienna Jacques

Vienna Jacques, daughter of Henry and Lucinda Jacques, was born on 10 June 1787 in Beverly, Essex, Massachusetts. She spent many of her adult years in Boston, where she used, in her words, "self-reliance, patient toil and strict economy" while working as a nurse to accumulate more than $1,400 (Hurd 63). Her life took a dramatic turn when she sent for a copy of the Book of Mormon. After reading this scripture and receiving a vision of its truthfulness, she was baptized in July 1832. Vienna moved to Ohio, and then to Jackson County, Missouri, to be with other Latter-day Saints. In Jackson County she consecrated her property to the Church and received an inheritance in Zion. Religious persecution forced her to flee from Missouri to Illinois, and then to the Salt Lake Valley. Vienna died on 7 February 1884 in Salt Lake City at the age of ninety-six.

Vienna's story, an exemplary model for modern Latter-day Saints, was dramatically retold by writer Jerrie Hurd. The life sketch includes Vienna's request for the Book of Mormon and the vision that caused her to forsake her profession in Boston and join with the Saints in Ohio.

❋   ❋   ❋

[Vienna Jacques] was a devout Christian and had associated with the Methodists, receiving "sanctification" as a member of the Broomfield Street church in Boston. But soon she became dissatisfied and began investigating several other Christian sects, seeking a church that evidenced the spiritual gifts described in the New Testament. Hearing of a new prophet in the West who had published a sacred record, she sent for the Book of Mormon and read it. At first she was unimpressed, but then late one evening as she walked home from a church meeting, she contemplated what the theme of her evening prayers should be. Suddenly she saw a vision of the Book of Mormon, and she resolved to ask about its truthfulness. Her conversion was not instantaneous but came gradually with continued study of the scriptures. As she tells it, after praying, she was able to more fully comprehend the book. She continued to read until her mind "was illuminated" and she became convinced of its divinity.

In 1831, traveling alone by canal and stagecoach, she made her way to Kirtland, Ohio. She described her journey to a reporter years later as "an arduous undertaking"; but she was "strong and concentrated in purpose, braving all danger and trusting in the Almighty for protection," and her way "was marvelously opened up."

In Kirtland, she met the Prophet and, after being further instructed, was baptized. She stayed in Ohio about six weeks and then returned to Boston, where she became the means of converting her mother, her sister, and her nieces, who were also baptized. They remained in the East, but Vienna was determined to join the Prophet and his other followers. She concluded her affairs in Boston, collected her valuables, and returned to Ohio, where, on March 8, 1833, she was instructed by revelation to give her money to the Church and settle in Missouri. (D&C 90:28-31.)

Vienna was in her mid-forties, past an age when most of her contemporaries would have considered giving up the security of a hard-earned nest egg to take up the uncertainties of life on the edge of the western frontier, especially as a lone woman. (From Hurd 63-64.)

Benjamin Franklin Johnson

Benjamin Franklin Johnson, son of Ezekiel Johnson and Julia Hills, was born on 28 July 1818 in Pomfret, Chautauqua,

Benjamin Franklin Johnson

New York. In 1835 he was baptized into the Church and soon moved to Kirtland, Ohio, to be with others of his faith. In 1838 he journeyed with the Kirtland Poor Camp to Missouri. He married Melissa Bloomfield on 25 December 1841, and they became the parents of eight children. On 18 December 1845 he received his endowment in the Nauvoo Temple. Benjamin is remembered for his service as private secretary to Joseph Smith, his missionary labors in the Sandwich Islands, and his membership in the Council of Fifty. He later resided in Utah, where in 1877 he became bishop of the Spring Lake Ward. Benjamin died on 18 November 1905 in Mesa, Maricopa, Arizona, at the age of eighty-seven.

Benjamin's personal history, My Life's Review, chronicles his first encounter with the "Golden Bible" at age thirteen. He vividly described his apprehensions about the Book of Mormon and his insatiable desire to learn more from its pages. His conversion story is filled with hope as he recognized that living prophets are upon the earth and that God had revealed to man this new, holy scripture.

※　※　※

About this time we began to hear more about the "Golden Bible" that had been found by "Joe Smith" the "money digger," etc., etc. My elder brother, David, having gone to visit Joel H. in Amherst, Ohio, had remained there until the next season, in the spring of which the first elders, going from Kirtland to Missouri, stopped and raised up a large branch of the Church into which both of my brothers were baptized. Previous to this, rumors had come from Ohio of the spread of what was called "Campbellism," a new sect, of which Sidney Rigdon was then the chief apostle, and through fear that my brothers would become deluded by the new doctrines, my mother had written a letter of caution to them, which was soon answered to say that they had both joined the "Mormonites" (then so called), believers in the Prophet Joseph Smith and the Book of Mormon or "Golden Bible." This news came upon us almost as a horror and a disgrace. The first news was soon followed by the Book of Mormon, accompanied by a lengthy explanation, on the receipt of which my mother, brother Seth, sister Nancy, and Lyman R. Sherman, with some of the neighbors, all devoted to religion, would meet together secretly to read the Book of Mormon and accompanying letter, or perhaps to deplore the delusion into which my brothers had fallen. But their reading soon led to marveling at the simplicity and purity of what they read, and at the spirit which accompanied it, bearing witness to its truth. After a few days of secrecy I was permitted to meet with them, to hear it read, being then 13 years of age; and in listening, a feeling of the most intense anxiety came over me to learn more. It seemed as if I must hear it all before I could be satisfied; and the principle of faith began to spring up in my heart to believe it. This was in the early fall of 1831. Now a bright hope began to arise in my heart that there really was a living prophet on the earth, and my greatest fear was that it would not prove true.

Later in the fall my brothers came from Ohio to see us and bear their testimony, and were accompanied by Almon W. Babbitt, then not seventeen years of age. They bore a faithful testimony, but neither of them seemed capable of teaching in a public capacity. As a family we were being converted to the truth, when unexpectedly there came to us Elders James [Joseph] Brackinbury and Jabez Durfee. Elder Brackinbury was a capable man and a great reasoner, and the Spirit of the Lord rested mightily upon him, confirming the words we had already received. My mother, and Lyman R. Sherman, my brother-in-law, were soon baptized, shortly followed by the baptism of all my brothers and sisters who had attained their majority. (From Benjamin F. Johnson 11-12.)

Joel Hills Johnson

Joel Hills Johnson, son of Ezekiel Johnson and Julia Hills, was born on 23 March 1802 in Grafton, Worcester, Massachusetts. He married Anna Pixley Johnson on 2 May 1826 in Pomfret, New York, and they became the parents of six children. On 1 June 1831 Joel was baptized, and on 20 September 1831 he was ordained an elder. Joel joined the persecuted Saints in Ohio, Missouri, Illinois, and the Salt Lake Valley. In the valley he served as a bishop, a stake president, and a patriarch. Joel died on 24 September 1882 in Johnson, Kane, Utah, at the age of eighty.

In his autobiography, Joel recalled his initial prejudices against the Book of Mormon. He then described how his attendance at Church meetings led him to read the Book of Mormon. His recitation encourages Latter-day Saints to logically support their own faith.

✻   ✻   ✻

About this time there was considerable excitement about the Mormons at Kirtland where there had been a branch of the church built up, and Joseph Smith had arrived at that place and held a conference and was sending out elders through the country; and many evil reports were in circulation concerning them which most of the people believed to be true. I obtained the Book of Mormon and read it. Some were filled with prejudice on account of the evil reports in circulation that I returned it before I had read it through. But soon there arrived two Mormon Elders in the neighborhood by the names of Marvey [Harvey] Whitlock and Edson Fuller who preached upon the first principles of the gospel, treating upon faith, repentance, and baptism for the remission of sins with the laying on of hands for the gift of the Holy Ghost, with signs following the believer, etc. This preaching filled me with astonishment, it being the first discourse that I had ever heard that corresponded with the New Testament. But when they spoke of the Book of Mormon, they made it equal to the Bible. But my prejudice was so great

In this Johnson family picture, Joel Hills Johnson is seated in the center, with Benjamin Franklin Johnson seated at right.

against the book, that I would not receive their testimony. I heard them twice and concluded to stay at home, but they continued preaching in the vicinity and soon commenced baptizing. In a few days Lyman Wright [Wight], Samuel H. Smith, and others came to their assistance, and in a few weeks they baptized about fifty in the vicinity.

All this time I had kept at home except for the first two meetings. My wife, who had always been a strong Methodist, had a desire at this time to attend their meetings which were held every day, and I gave my consent, for I never would abridge one's liberty in religious matters. She attended several meetings and began to believe in the work, and myself having searched the Bible daily while staying at home, began to think that work might possibly be true. I therefore concluded to adhere to the advice of Paul "to prove all things and hold fast the good." I accordingly came to the conclusion to take my Bible in hand and attend all their meetings and investigate any subject thoroughly with prayer for Divine direction which I did for several days, comparing their preachings with the scriptures which brought me to the following conclusions: Firstly, that as all Protestant sects had sprung from the Church of Rome, they have no more authority to administer in the ordinances of the Church of Christ than the Church of Rome had, and if she was the mother of harlots, they must consequently be her daughters; therefore, none of them could be called the Church of Christ. Secondly, that a supernatural power did attend the Mormon Church, and it had risen independent of all denominations; therefore, its origin must be from heaven or hell. Thirdly, that it is unreasonable to suppose that God would suffer the devil to bring forth a work with the gifts and blessings of the ancient Church of Christ corresponding with that which he has promised to bring forth in the last days for the gathering of the House of Israel and by that means lead astray all the honest men of the earth. And fourthly, that as the principles taught in the Book of Mormon corresponded with the Bible and doctrine of the Church was the same that was taught by Christ and his apostles with signs following the believer, I concluded that the work was of God and embraced with all my heart and soul, and was baptized on the first day of June 1831, by Elder Sylvester Smith. My wife had been baptized a few days previous.

I then immediately sold out of my share in the sawmill and endeavored to prepare myself for whatever my calling might be, and on the 24th of August, 1831, I was ordained a teacher; and on the 20th of September 1831, I was ordained an Elder. (From Joel Hills Johnson 3-4.)

Mary Elizabeth Rollins Lightner

Mary Lightner, daughter of John Porter Rollins and Keziah Keturah Van Benthuysen, was born on 9 April 1818 in Lima, Livingston, New York. When she was ten years old, she moved to Kirtland, Ohio, to live with her uncle, Algernon Gilbert. Mary resided with the Gilberts for two years before hearing about the Book of Mormon from traveling missionaries. She described their message: "They bore a powerful testimony, by the Holy Spirit, of the truth of the great work they were engaged in; and which they were commissioned by the Father to present to all the world" ("Mary Elizabeth Rollins Lightner" 193).

Mary was baptized in October 1830, and in 1831 she moved to Jackson County, Missouri, where she witnessed many scenes of mob violence. She and her sister, Caroline, were able to save

Mary Elizabeth Rollins Lightner

pages of the Book of Commandments from being burned by "get-ting our arms full" and hiding in the cornfield to avoid detection. Later she wrote, "They got them bound in small books and sent me one, which I prized very highly" ("Mary Elizabeth Rollins Lightner" 196). On 11 August 1835 she married Adam Lightner, a resident of Clay County. They endured continual persecution until they moved away from the gathering places of the Saints. It was not until 1863 that she crossed the plains to settle in Min-ersville, Utah. Mary died on 17 December 1917 at the age of ninety-nine.

In July 1926, a brief sketch of Mary's early life in Ohio ap-peared in the Utah Genealogical and Historical Magazine. *In the article, she described how she borrowed a copy of the Book of Mormon from Isaac Morley and soon gained a testimony of its truthfulness.*

✻   ✻   ✻

About this time, John Whitmer came and brought a Book of Mormon. There was a meeting that evening, and we learned that Brother Morley had the Book in his possession—the only one in that part of the country. I went to his house just before the meeting was to commence, and asked to see the Book; Brother Morley put it in my hand, as I looked at it, I felt such a desire to read it, that I could not refrain from asking him to let me take it home and read it, while he attended meeting. He said it would be too late for me to take it back after meeting, and another thing, he had hardly had time to read a chapter in it himself, and but few of the brethren had even seen it, but I plead so earnestly for it, he finally said, "child, if you will bring this book home before breakfast tomorrow morning, you may take it." He admonished me to be very careful, and see that no harm came to it. If any person in this world was ever perfectly happy in the possession of any coveted treasure I was when I had permission to read that wonderful book. Uncle [Algernon Sidney Gilbert] and Aunt were Methodists, so when I got into the house, I exclaimed, "Oh, Uncle, I have got the 'Golden Bible'." Well, there was consternation in the house for a few moments, and I was severely reprimanded for being so presumtious [*sic*] as to ask such a favor, when Brother Morley had not read it himself. However, we all took turns reading it until very late in the night—as soon as it was light enough to see, I was up and learned the first verse in the book. When I reached Brother Morley's they had been up for only a little while. When I handed him the book, he remarked, "I guess you did not read much in it." I showed him how far we had read. He was surprised, and said, "I don't believe you can tell me one word of it." I then repeated the first verse, also the outlines of the history of Nephi. He gazed at me in surprise, and said, "child, take this book home and finish it, I can wait." Before or about the time I finished the last chapter, the Prophet Joseph Smith arrived in Kirtland, and moved into a part of Newel K. Whitney's house, (Uncle Algernon's partner in the Mercantile Business), while waiting for his goods to be put in order. Brother Whitney brought the Prophet Joseph to our house and introduced him to the older ones of the family. (I was not in at the time.) In looking around he saw the Book of Mormon on the shelf, and asked how that book came to be there. He said, "I sent that book to Brother Morley." Uncle told him how his niece had obtained it. He asked, "Where is your niece?" I was sent for; when he saw me he looked at me so earnestly, I felt almost afraid. After a moment or two he came and put his hands on my head and gave me a great blessing, the first I ever received, and made me a present of the book, and said he would give Brother Morley another. (From "Mary Elizabeth Rollins Lightner" 194-95.)

Missionaries to the Lamanites

At the conclusion of his mission to the Lamanites, Parley P. Pratt reported that Ziba Peterson, Peter Whitmer, Jr., Oliver Cowdery, and he himself "had preached the gospel in its fulness, and distributed the record of their forefathers among three tribes" (44). Parley's most detailed report focused on their missionary activities among the Delawares in western Missouri. He described attending an Indian council presided over by Chief Anderson, the grand sachem of ten tribes.

Before the missionaries arrived, the chief had opposed all Christian missionary work among his tribes. However, through an interpreter, the brethren boldly asked to be heard before a full Indian council. After lengthy consideration, a runner was dispatched to the tribes, and forty leading men were assembled. At the request of Chief Anderson, Oliver Cowdery delivered the first address. His speech and Chief Anderson's response have been preserved in the official history of the Church. The moving yet simple address concerning the value of the Book of Mormon to the Indians, and the chief's humble reply, reaffirm our faith.

✻   ✻   ✻

Oliver Cowdery's Address to the Indian Council

"Aged Chief, and Venerable Council of the Delaware nation: we are glad of this opportunity to address you as our red brethren and friends. We have traveled a long distance from towards the rising sun to bring you glad news; we have traveled the wilderness, crossed the deep and wide rivers, and waded in the deep snows, and in the face of the storms of winter, to communicate to you great knowledge which has lately come to our ears and hearts and which will do the red man good as well as the pale face.

"Once the red men were many; they occupied the country from sea to sea—from the rising to the setting sun; the whole land was theirs; the Great Spirit gave it to them, and no pale faces dwelt among them. But now they are few in numbers;

their possessions are small, and the pale faces are many.

"Thousands of moons ago, when the red men's forefathers dwelt in peace and possessed this whole land, the Great Spirit talked with them, and revealed His law and His will, and much knowledge to their wise men and prophets. This they wrote in a Book, together with their history and the things which should befall their children in the latter days.

"This Book was written on plates of gold and handed down from father to son for many ages and generations.

"It was then that the people prospered and were strong and mighty; they cultivated the earth, built buildings and cities and abounded in all good things, as the pale faces now do.

"But they became wicked; they killed one another and shed much blood; they killed their prophets and wise men, and sought to destroy the Book. The Great Spirit became angry and would speak to them no more; they had no more good and wise dreams; no more visions; no more angels sent among them by the Great Spirit; and the Lord commanded Mormon and Moroni, their last wise men and prophets to hide the Book in the earth, that it might be preserved in safety and be found and made known in the latter-day to the pale faces who should possess the land, that they might again make it known to the red men, in order to restore them to the knowledge of the will of the Great Spirit and to His favor. And if the red men would then receive this Book and learn the things written in it and do according thereunto, they should be restored to all their rights and privileges; should cease to fight and kill one another; should become one people; cultivate the earth in peace, in common with the pale faces, who were willing to believe and obey the same Book and be good men and live in peace.

"Then should the red men become great and have plenty to eat and good clothes to wear, and should be in favor with the Great Spirit and be His children, while He would be their Great Father and talk with them, and raise up prophets and wise and good men among them again, who should teach them many things.

"This Book, which contained these things, was hid in the earth by Moroni, in a hill called by him Cumorah, which hill is now in the State of New York, near the village of Palmyra, in Ontario county.

"In that neighborhood there lived a young man named Joseph Smith, who prayed to the Great Spirit much, in order that he might know the truth, and the Great Spirit sent an angel to him and told him where this Book was hid by Moroni, and commanded him to go and get it. He accordingly went to the place and dug in the earth and found the Book written on golden plates.

"But it was written in the language of the forefathers of the red men; therefore this young man, being a pale face, could not understand it; but the angel told him and showed him and gave him knowledge of the language and how to interpret the Book. So he interpreted it into the language of the pale faces, and wrote it on paper and caused it to be printed, and published thousands of copies of it among them, and then sent us to the red men to bring some copies of it to them, and to tell them this news. So we have now come from him, and here is a copy of the Book, which we now present to our red friend, the Chief of the Delawares, which we hope he will cause to be read and known among his tribe; it will do them good." (Qtd. in Joseph Smith, *History of the Church* 1:183-84n.)

Chief Anderson's Reply

After the Book of Mormon was presented to the chief, there was a brief pause while the Indian council talked among themselves. Chief Anderson then spoke:

"We feel truly thankful to our white friends who have come so far and been at such pains to tell us good news, and especially this new news concerning the Book of our forefathers; it makes us glad in here"—placing his hand on his heart. "It is now winter; we are new settlers in this place; the snow is deep; our cattle and horses are dying; our wigwams are poor; we have much to do in the spring—to build houses and fence and make farms; but we will build a council house and meet together, and you shall read to us and teach us more concerning the Book of our fathers and the will of the Great Spirit." (Qtd. in Joseph Smith, *History of the Church* 1:184-85n.)

David Pettegrew

David Pettegrew, son of William Pettegrew and Phebe Hardy, was born on 29 July 1791 in Weathersfield, Windsor, Vermont.

He married Elizabeth Alden, and they became the parents of seven children. In 1832 he was baptized into the Church by Isaac Higbee and moved to Ohio, and later to Missouri, to be with other Latter-day Saints. In the fall of 1838, David was persecuted and imprisoned in the Richmond jail. He fled from religious intolerance in Missouri to Illinois, where he served on the Nauvoo High Council. He marched with the Mormon Battalion from Council Bluffs to Ciudad de los Angeles and was considered the father figure of the battalion. After his discharge he served as bishop of the Salt Lake City 10th Ward from 1849 to 1863. David died on 31 December 1863 in Salt Lake City at the age of seventy-two.

During the later years of his life, David wrote an autobiography describing his early days in the Church. He detailed his first impression of the Latter-day Saint faith and told how the Book of Mormon led him to embrace the gospel of Jesus Christ.

❋   ❋   ❋

And thus I passed my days until, the year eighteen hundred and thirty one, when I felt more convinced that some great event was at hand, but what it would be I could not divine, but my prayers to my God was that I might know his ways and his will concerning the sons of men. On the first day of the year thirty-two, as I was reading in my room, before prayers, some person knocked at my door, I bid him to walk in and behold, it was a man whom I had had some acquaintance with some years before, which I considered a just and upright man, but not very intelligent, I enquired what was the news, and what sect[s] were doing the most in the cause of religion, he answered that the Methodist[s] he thought were doing the best of any. We conversed a while upon different topics, and at length he asked me if I had heard of a people called the Mormons. I replied that I never had only from what I had read in the Christian's Advocate, printed at New York. I there read some slurs about a people that were gathering in the upper part of the state of Missouri, and supposed they were a fit people for the penitentiary. I asked him if he knew anything about them, to which he replied that he did and believed them to be a good people and that he had a book of their religion upon which I asked him to let me see it, and he handed me the Book of Mormon, this was indeed new to me, and I thought a trick, as he looked upon this book, as sacred as on the Bible. I opened the

book, it was the second book of Nephi, and the fifth chapter. I
read on awhile my thoughts were very active, what to think I
knew not: It was entirely a new thing to me and I began to mind
what I was reading, although I observed to my wife that I did
not think that it was the words of him that had a devil. This
was on the Sabbath morning, I read until meeting time, I then
invited the gentleman to meeting house, the people had gathered together for meeting. I informed the congregation that this
gentleman that was with me was a professor of religion, and if it
was their desire that he should occupy the pulpit the forenoon,
there was no objection, and he opened the meeting with
prayers, and then read the twenty ninth chapter of Isaiah, and,
then spoke of the Book of Mormon and that God had brought it
forth, by raising up a prophet and it was the fullness of the everlasting gospel, and after he had spoken what he saw fit he sat
down, and I immediately arose and spoke as follows, brethren
there has been certainly strange things come to our ears, that
we had not thought of, which is entirely new to us, therefore, I
recommend that we be wise and not hasty in making up our
minds concerning this matter, for if it is of man, it will be good
for nothing and will soon come to naught, but if it should be of
God, and we should be found at variance with it, we would be
exceedingly sorry in days to come. I know not whether it is of
God or of man, but this much I do know, that there is no harm
in being wise in these things, and took my seat. Neighbor
Beach, Esq., arose and said strange delusion. We read that
strange things will take place in the last days, and here they are
already amongst us, it is intolerable to think or suppose that
such could be the fact. It is blasphemy in the highest, and as-
tonishing to think that a man possessed with the least common
sense should think to be imposed upon in this manner, high
delusion, it is for us all to awake or we shall be grossly deceived, he took his seat, and I took notice as he spoke that he
was much excited, for he trembled and looked angry. I saw that
we were about to have confusion, and I called the class to
order, and spoke to the class as usual, and soon after dismissed them, the gentleman of the Mormon Church went on
his way and in a few weeks returned again. I now made up my
mind to purchase from him the Book of Mormon, which I did
and intended to read it through and keep it to myself. I soon
found that the report of my purchase had spread abroad like
wild fire, the news rolled around the circuit, that Brother Pette-

grew was ruined, and it was fearful he would be lost. Soon the preacher came who had charge of our circuit, his name was Oglesby, he took his text in the third chapter, first verse in Galatians. O foolish Galatians who hath bewitched you that you should not obey the truth. He labored diligently to show the danger of believing any other gospel, or anything else but the Holy Bible, and remarked that if an angel, or a plenipotentiary should descend from heaven with any other gospel, than we had in the Bible, he would say let him be accursed and God would say let him be accursed and Paul would say let him be accursed, and thus he warned us from the Book of Mormon. I persuaded him to take the book with him around the circuit and read it, and I requested him to note all the places that he should find contrary to the gospel of the Bible and bring them to me, which he promised to do. Upon his return the second time, I enquired of him if he had read the book, to which he answered, no brother Pettegrew, it is not worth reading, it is the most unmeaning thing I ever read. I can show you in a minute (and began to look to find the places, but could not find but one) and that was concerning the hundred and sixteen pages, he thought that if they had been translated once, it might easily be done again, but he too soon saw his mistake and Satan had put it into their hearts to change the words that it should not read the same. The time had now arrived for public preaching, and took his text in the second chapter of Isaiah, and the last verse. And in that day, a man shall cast his idols of silver and his idols of gold, which every one of them had made for himself to worship to the moles and to the bats, to go into to the cliffs of the rocks and into the tops of the cragged rocks for fear of the Lord, and for the glory of his majesty, when he ariseth to shake terribly the earth, cease ye from man whose breath is in his nostrils, for wherewith is he to be accounted of. Thus was the foundation which he took to build his sermon upon, and after he had gotten through with his sermon he then exclaimed, Brother Pettegrew, I now exhort you to call in your neighbors and take your Book of Mormon and burn it a sacrifice to old Moloch and let all witness the sight. This gave me peculiar feelings to see a man in the high standing of Doctor Oglesby to treat so lightly upon things which I knew he did not understand. I thought then, poor man, he will want to be first into the tops of the cragged rocks, to hide from the glory of his majesty when he ariseth to shake terribly the earth. I cried unto the

Lord for help and give the understanding which would guide me to my duty, and that I might get rid of my office in the class, for my mind was now enlightened and I thought it would not do for me to partake of the sacrament administered in the Methodist Church as formerly. I kept this to myself and pondered well over these things in my heart. Soon after, I was advised by Doctor Oglesby to withdraw from the class. My place in the class was soon filled by another and I was accordingly released, to my heart's desire, and was loosed from the church without any difficulty on my part. These things caused me to draw nearer to the Lord, and he to me and he witnessed to me that he had now began his work for the last days, and that the Book of Mormon was the true book and by it I saw that the Lord was the same Lord, and its gospel was the same and its ordinances were the same as those I had been thought to observe. But man, poor man had changed or transgressed the law, changed the ordinances, and had broken the everlasting covenant, and yet the Lord had spared the earth notwithstanding the many ways, parties, and sects, we had been divided into, and yet none right; but all had gone astray. I truly saw that God was of long suffering and of much patience. My heart was poured out in prayer to my God, and the solemnity of eternity rested upon my mind. . . . I, therefore, searched the prophesies and I plainly saw that there was much yet to be fulfilled, and the world was still in the dark as regarded this matter, and my heart was pained and weighed down with sorrow because of the gross darkness that covered the minds of the people. . . . I saw that the days of my peace and enjoyment were over if I remained at my place of residence. I, therefore, resolved to change my location. I had heard that the people that believed in the Book of Mormon were gathering in the upper part of the state of Missouri, thither I was determined to go. (From Pettegrew, Journal 1–4.)

William Wines Phelps

William Wines Phelps, son of Enon Phelps and Mehitable Goldsmith, was born on 17 February 1792 in Hanover, Morris, New Jersey. He married Stella Waterman on 28 April 1815 in Smyrna, New York, and they became the parents of eleven children. The sacred contents of the Book of Mormon led him to abandon his editing and political professions in New York and

William Wines Phelps

seek religious haven with the persecuted Mormons in Ohio. On 10 June 1831 he was baptized in Kirtland, Ohio. From 1834 to 1838 he served in the Presidency of the Church in Missouri. In our generation he is most remembered for his hymns, "The Spirit of God" and "Praise to the Man." William died on 6 March 1872 in Salt Lake City at the age of eighty.

In an editorial appearing in the Latter Day Saints' Messenger and Advocate, *William wrote of the knowledge contained in the Book of Mormon: "It is a good book and no honest person can read it, without feeling grateful to God, for the knowledge it contains" (177, emphasis in original). He then penned his reaction to reading the Book of Mormon.*

❀　　❀　　❀

From the first time I read this volume of volumes, even till now, I have been struck with a kind of sacred joy at its title page. . . .

. . . What a wonderful volume! what a glorious treasure! By that book I learned the right way to God; by that book I received the fulness of the everlasting gospel; by that book I found the new covenant; by that book I learned . . . that the new Jerusalem, even Zion was to be built up on this continent; by that book I found a key to the holy prophets; and by that book began to unfold the mysteries of God, and I was made glad. Who can tell his goodness, or estimate the worth of such a book? He only who is directed by the Holy Ghost in all things, and has kept all his Lord's commandments blameless through life.

. . . The book of Mormon, is just what it was when it first came forth—a revelation from the Lord. The knowledge it contains is desirable; the doctrine it teaches is from the blessed Savior; its precepts are good; its principles righteous; its judgments just; its style simple, and its language plain: so that a way-faring man, though a fool, need not err therein.

. . . If the majority of mankind would give as much credit to the statements of their fellow beings who certify to the truth of this book, as they do to the foolish lies that are put in circulation by wretches of no character, they would believe it upon testimony. Not a few, then, but thousands, would rejoice and say, truth is light, and light comes from God. (From William W. Phelps 177–78.)

Parley Parker Pratt

Parley Parker Pratt, son of Jared Pratt and Charity Dickinson, was born on 12 April 1807 in Burlington, Otsego, New York. He married Thankful Halsey on 9 September 1827 in Canaan, New York, and they became the parents of one child. Parley's conversion to the Church began when he read the Book of Mormon. The Spirit which wrought upon him during his first reading was so powerful that eating and sleeping became a burden. On 1 September 1830 Parley was baptized in Seneca Lake by Oliver Cowdery. The new convert commenced preaching the restored truths of the Book of Mormon the next Sunday and was so convincing that four families requested baptism immediately following his sermon. From 1835 to 1857 he was a member of the Council of the Twelve Apostles. Parley was assassinated on 13 May 1857 in Van Buren, Crawford, Arkansas, at the age of fifty.

Parley described his life of dedicated service in his autobiography, which is often used as a primary source for describing the

Parley Parker Pratt

powerful influence of the Book of Mormon. While visiting an el-
derly baptist deacon named Hamlin, he was told of a strange
new book—a book that was to bring everlasting joy to the inquis-
itive Parley.

❉   ❉   ❉

This book, [Hamlin] said, purported to have been originally
written on plates either of gold or brass, by a branch of the
tribes of Israel; and to have been discovered and translated by a
young man near Palmyra, in the State of New York, by the aid
of visions, or the ministry of angels. I inquired of him how or
where the book was to be obtained. He promised me the perusal of it, at his house the next day, if I would call. I felt a
strange interest in the book. I preached that evening to a small
audience, who appeared to be interested in the truths which I
endeavored to unfold to them in a clear and lucid manner from
the Scriptures. Next morning I called at his house, where, for
the first time, my eyes beheld the "BOOK OF MORMON"—that
book of books—that record which reveals the antiquities of the

"New World" back to the remotest ages, and which unfolds the destiny of its people and the world for all time to come;—that Book which contains the fulness of the gospel of a crucified and risen Redeemer;—that Book which reveals a lost remnant of Joseph, and which was the principal means, in the hands of God, of directing the entire course of my future life.

I opened it with eagerness, and read its title page. I then read the testimony of several witnesses in relation to the manner of its being found and translated. After this I commenced its contents by course. I read all day; eating was a burden, I had no desire for food; sleep was a burden when the night came, for I preferred reading to sleep.

As I read, the spirit of the Lord was upon me, and I knew and comprehended that the book was true, as plainly and manifestly as a man comprehends and knows that he exists. My joy was now full, as it were, and I rejoiced sufficiently to more than pay me for all the sorrows, sacrifices and toils of my life. I soon determined to see the young man who had been the instrument of its discovery and translation. . . .

This discovery greatly enlarged my heart, and filled my soul with joy and gladness. I esteemed the Book, or the information contained in it, more than all the riches of the world. Yes; I verily believe that I would not at that time have exchanged the knowledge I then possessed, for a legal title to all the beautiful farms, houses, villages and property which passed in review before me, on my journey through one of the most flourishing settlements of western New York. (From Pratt 19-20, 22.)

Willard Richards

Willard Richards, son of Joseph Richards and Rhoda Howe, was born on 24 June 1804 in Hopkinton, Middlesex, Massachusetts. In 1814 he and his family moved to Richmond, Massachusetts, where he often attended sectarian revivals. These revivals convinced ten-year-old Willard that religious sects "were all wrong and that God had no Church on the earth." However, he possessed a youthful hope that the Lord would "soon have a church whose creed would be the truth, and nothing but the truth." As this hope matured through two decades, Willard kept himself aloof from sectarianism, but did not hesitate to "boldly declar[e] his belief to all who wished to learn his views, until the

Willard Richards

summer of 1835." (Green 61.) That summer, he read the Book of Mormon and soon requested membership in the Church.

On 31 December 1836 Willard was baptized in Kirtland, Ohio, by his cousin Brigham Young. He served a mission in the eastern states before preaching the restored gospel in England. During his mission to England he married Jennetta Richards on 24 September 1838, and they became the parents of three children. On 14 April 1840 Willard was ordained a member of the Council of the Twelve Apostles. From 1847 to 1854 he served as Second Counselor to Brigham Young in the First Presidency of the Church. Willard died on 11 March 1854 in Salt Lake City at the age of forty-nine.

Willard's testimony of the Church began when he was given a copy of the Book of Mormon by Brigham Young. Before receiving this book, he had seen scurrilous public newspaper accounts claiming that "a boy named Joe Smith, somewhere out west, had found a Gold Bible" (Green 61). This book was to change the course of his life. An account of Willard's experience appears in the book Testimonies of Our Leaders.

❋　❋　❋

[Willard] opened the book, without regard to place, and totally ignorant of its design or contents, and before reading half a page, declared that, "God or the devil has had a hand in that book, for man never wrote it." He read it twice through in about ten days; and so firm was his conviction of the truth, that he immediately commenced settling his accounts, selling his medicine, and freeing himself from every incumbrance, that he might go to Kirtland, Ohio, seven hundred miles west, the nearest point he could hear of a Saint, and give the work a thorough investigation; firmly believing that if the doctrine was true, God had some greater work for him to do than peddle pills. But no sooner did he commence a settlement, than he was smitten with the palsy, from which he suffered exceedingly, and was prevented executing his design, until October, 1836, when he arrived at Kirtland, in company with his brother (Doctor Levi Richards, who attended him as physician), where he was most cordially and hospitably received and entertained by his cousin, Brigham Young, with whom he tarried, and gave the work an unceasing and untiring investigation, until December 31, 1836, when he was baptized by Brigham Young, at Kirtland. (From Green 61-62.)

Sidney Rigdon

Sidney Rigdon, son of William Rigdon and Nancy Galliger, was born on 19 February 1793 in Allegheny County, Pennsylvania. At age twenty-five he obtained a preaching license and soon was addressing large congregations at the First Baptist Church in Pittsburgh, Pennsylvania. He married Phebe Brook on 12 June 1820, and they became the parents of eleven children. As Sidney's familiarity with the Bible grew, he became perplexed about the doctrines he was asked to preach to the Baptists. He perceived a marked difference between Baptist beliefs and biblical teachings.

In 1823 Sidney withdrew from the Baptist church and joined with Alexander Campbell in founding the Campbellite faith. By the fall of 1830, Sidney had left this faith to continue his search for the pure doctrine of Christ. That year, Parley P. Pratt, an old acquaintance of Sidney's, introduced him to the Book of Mormon. Although skeptical at first, he became convinced of its truth through prayerfully reading its contents. Sidney was baptized on 14 November 1830 in Ohio. From 1833 to 1844 he served as a

Sidney Rigdon

counselor to Joseph Smith in the First Presidency of the Church. After the Prophet's martyrdom, Sidney desired to be guardian of the Church. When his claims of leadership were dismissed, he established his own church in Pittsburgh, with the Book of Mormon as a partial basis for belief. Sidney died on 14 July 1876 in Friendship, New York, at the age of eighty-three.

An account of Sidney's prayerful search of the Book of Mormon is written in the official history of the Church. These recollections reveal the stirring testimony of this book which he maintained throughout his life. To him, the Book of Mormon contained the doctrines he had sought since his earliest days in Pennsylvania.

❋   ❋   ❋

The first house at which they [Oliver Cowdery, Parley P. Pratt, and their fellow missionaries] called in the vicinity of Kirtland, was Mr. Rigdon's, and after the usual salutations, they presented him with the Book of Mormon, stating that it was a revelation from God. This being the first time he had ever heard of, or seen, the Book of Mormon, he felt very much surprised at

the assertion, and replied that he had the Bible which he believed was a revelation from God, and with which he pretended
to have some acquaintance; but with respect of the book they
had presented him, he must say that he had considerable
doubt. Upon this, they expressed a desire to investigate the
subject, and argue the matter. But he replied, "No, young gentlemen, you must not argue with me on the subject; but I will
read your book, and see what claims it has upon my faith, and
will endeavor to ascertain whether it be a revelation from God
or not."

After some further conversation they expressed a desire to
lay the subject before the people, and requested the privilege of
preaching in Mr. Rigdon's chapel, to which he readily con-
sented. The appointment was accordingly published, and a
large and respectable congregation assembled. Oliver Cowdery
and Parley P. Pratt severally addressed the meeting. At the conclusion, Mr. Rigdon arose, and stated to the congregation that
the information they had that evening received was of an extraordinary character, and certainly demanded their most serious consideration; and as the Apostle advised his brethren to
"prove all things, and hold fast that which is good," so he would
exhort his brethren to do likewise, and give the matter a careful
investigation, and not turn against it without being fully convinced of its being an imposition, lest they should, possibly, re-
sist the truth.

A few miles from Mr. Rigdon's home in Mentor, at the town
of Kirtland, lived a number of the members of his church. They
lived together and had all things common—from which circum-
stance has risen the idea that this was the case with the
Church of Jesus Christ. To that place the Elders immediately
repaired, and proclaimed the Gospel unto them, with considerable success; for their testimony was received by many of the
people, and seventeen came forward in obedience to the Gospel.

While thus engaged, they visited Mr. Rigdon occasionally,
and found him very earnestly reading the Book of Mormon,—
praying to the Lord for direction, and meditating on the things
he heard and read; and after a fortnight from the time the book
was put into his hands, he was fully convinced of the truth of
the work, by a revelation from Jesus Christ, which was made
known to him in a remarkable manner, so that he could ex-
claim, "Flesh and blood hath not revealed it unto me, but my
Father which is in heaven." Accordingly he and his wife were

both baptized into the Church of Jesus Christ; and, together with those who had previously admitted to baptism, made a little branch of the Church, in this section of Ohio, of about twenty members. (From Joseph Smith, *History of the Church* 1:122-25.)

Luman Andros Shurtliff

Luman Shurtliff, son of Noah Shurtliff and Lydia Brown, was born on 13 March 1807 in Montgomery, Hampden, Massachusetts. He married Eunice Gaylord on 4 July 1830, and they became the parents of eight children. In 1836 Luman was baptized into the Church by Sylvester Pitt and soon moved to Kirtland, Ohio. He served many proselyting missions in the midwest states, including Ohio, Michigan, and Indiana. In Illinois, Luman was a member of the Nauvoo Legion. In 1851 he migrated to the Salt Lake Valley and settled in Weber County. Luman died on 25 August 1884 in Harrisville, Weber, Utah, at the age of seventy-seven.

In his autobiography Luman recalled his search for the true gospel. His descriptive narrative tells of his struggle with moods of evil skepticism. His struggle ended with a powerful testimony of Joseph Smith and the Book of Mormon.

✻   ✻   ✻

I promised the Lord if he would show me the way and give me knowledge of the true gospel I would preach it as long as I lived. In the sincerity of my heart, I made this covenant time and again. One morning in August, 1836, I told my wife I thought I would make a trip to Kirtland, the seat of Mormonism and see if I could find out the truth or falsity of this doctrine from there.

I started on my journey on foot, and when I called on my folks in Franklin and told my relatives that I was going to Kirtland, my folks were silent, except father, and he said he was glad I was going, for Mormonism had troubled me for a long time and he hoped I would be satisfied. This somewhat encouraged me. After I had spent a few days in Franklin, I went to Kirtland.

I was a stranger there except for a Mr. Packard who had been at my house in Franklin, but I knew nothing of where he lived. As I passed the Kirtland Temple, I inquired of some boys for Noah Packard. They said they were his boys and would go with me to their home. Mr. Packard was gone on a mission. Mrs. Packard was a cousin of mine by marriage, but I had never seen her. She received me very kindly. . . .

The next morning I was up early and looked over the city of the Mormons. In the afternoon a funeral sermon was delivered in the temple by Jared Carter, a smart speaker, but I learned nothing in particular. The fact was the horizon of my mind was so obscured by clouds of darkness and doubt of long standing that I could see nothing as I ought.

The evil spirit came upon me and had that power over me that at times I would shake like a man with the ague. At another time I would be standing on some emenance weeping like a whipped child, and knew no reason why; then lost in meditation, wandering about the city like a man of little sense.

While in this situation, my tormentor whispered in my mind and said my little boy Lewis was dead and if I did not go home immediately he would be buried and I would not see him more. I then called to mind that the babe was not quite well the morning I left as usual. This strengthened or confirmed the whispering of that spirit and in spite of all my effort to the contrary, it much troubled my mind. . . . Well, I was in Kirtland with this [crippled] leg and it was getting worse fast, and it appeared if I stayed a day or so, I might be obliged to stay some time, and if my boy was dead, I might see him no more.

Thus, Saturday night found me a poor miserable man. Sunday I went to meeting. There I found a man by the name of Hyrum Daton [Hiram Dayton] with whom I had a slight acquaintance some years before. I told him I had come to Kirtland to learn the truth of Mormonism, and I had learned nothing new. I should return tomorrow and trouble my head no more about Mormonism. Yet, I would like to see and have a chat with some of the leading men before I left. Mr. Daton kindly offered to go with me to Brother David Whitmer and give me an introduction to him. As all of the higher officers were absent, I thought this would be my best way of learning what I wanted to know, and as Mr. Whitmer was one of the witnesses of the Book of Mormon, I thought I could learn something.

We walked to Mr. Whitmer's. I got the necessary introduction and took dinner and spent the afternoon in hearing him relate things about the Angel showing him the plates from which

the Book of Mormon was translated. I also asked him all the
questions I had a wish to ask. I had read and heard it all and
learned nothing new.

When tired of sitting, we walked out to where we could
overlook the flats, where I told him briefly in as few words as
possible, my belief and unbelief. I said I did believe the Gospel
they preached as far as I read it in the Bible, but I could not say
that I believed that Joseph Smith, Jr. was a true prophet of God
for I did not. Neither did I believe the Book of Mormon to be a
revelation from God, for I did not. Then facing him I said, "Now
you know what I believe and what I do not believe, and if you
think I am a fit subject for baptism, I am ready to go to the
water; if not, I intend to start home tomorrow and never trouble
my head any more about Mormonism."

Mr. Whitmer was silent a few seconds and then replied, "I
will go to the water and baptize you or get one of my quorum to
do it." On the way to the river, he called on Sylvester Smith and
at sunset Sunday, August 21, 1836, I was baptized a member
of the Church. David Whitmer confirmed me.

I felt very comfortable and at ease. I slept well that night
and in the morning I went to the office and bought a Book of
Mormon and started home. I had not traveled far when my leg
became worse and the pain severe. I had to walk slow. Upon reflection I saw it must be three or four days before I could get
home, and if my boy was sick he might die.

I knew my neighbors would ask me questions as soon as I
got home, and what could I tell them? I could tell them I had
been baptized and confirmed a member of the Church and
what evidence have I attained more than I had years ago? Not
any. Have I received the Holy Ghost since I was baptized? No.
No more than when I was baptized before. Did I believe the
Book of Mormon? No. No more than I did four years ago. Do I
believe that Joseph Smith, Jr. is a prophet of God? No, I do not.
At this I was shocked at my situation and began to call on the
Lord in earnest.

While I was praying, something came on my head resem-
bling cold water and passed gradually down through my whole
system, removing all pain, and made me a sound man from the
top of my head to the soles of my feet.

As soon as this was passed, I heard a sweet melodious voice
about me say, "Joseph Smith, Jr. is a prophet of the Most High
God, raised up for the restoration of Israel in these last days,

and the Book of Mormon which you hold under your arm is true and brought forth for the restoration of the scattered remnants of Jacob."

As this passed off, I cast my eyes to the south. A little way from me I saw my wife standing with my little boy sitting on her left arm with the right arm on her left shoulder and with her right hand pointing to me as if she was saying, "See father, there is father." They both were well and all right. This passed, I was in the road, a sound man, praising God.

After a few miles I began to think what I would say to my neighbors when I got home. I would tell them I knew the Mormon doctrine was true and I had seen and knew much and could do something great. . . .

On arriving home, I found all well and I thanked God continually for His forbearance and great mercy and long suffering in sparing my life to the present time, even after I had rejected the testimony that I had asked of him and at last, after four years, condescended to make known to me the trust of that great work. Thanks be to God for his goodness to me!

My neighbors were as still as a summer's morning. I had been a cripple there with them three years and they knew and saw it. I was now among them, sound and a healthy man. I was weighed down with sorrow and fettered with affliction. I now rejoiced in the Lord and my soul was full of joy, and my neighbors seemed to mourn. (From Shurtliff, "Biographical Sketch.")

George Albert Smith

George Albert Smith, son of John Smith and Clarissa Loomis Lyman, was born on 26 June 1817 in Potsdam, St. Lawrence, New York. He attended the Congregational Church until the winter of 1828, when his father received a letter from Joseph Smith, Jr., prophesying that awful judgments awaited the wicked. George was deeply impressed by the letter and by his father's exclamation, "Joseph writes like a Prophet!" (Qtd. in Jenson 1:38.) On 10 September 1832 George was baptized in Potsdam by Joseph H. Wakefield. After his baptism he served missions in Ohio, New York, Pennsylvania, and England.

From 1839 to 1863, George was a member of the Council of the Twelve Apostles. He married Bathsheba Wilson Bigler on 25 July 1841 in Nauvoo, Illinois, and they became the parents of

George Albert Smith

three children. They settled in Salt Lake City, where George served as Church Historian and General Recorder and as First Counselor to President Brigham Young. George died on 1 September 1875 in Salt Lake City at the age of fifty-eight.

His defense of the Book of Mormon throughout his many years of Church service was strong and renowned. He often cited an August 1830 visit from his uncle, Joseph Smith, Sr., and his cousin, Don Carlos Smith, as the beginning point of his testimony. They left a copy of the Book of Mormon with their relatives, then continued their journey to St. Lawrence, New York, to visit the ailing patriarch, Asael Smith. George and his mother read much in the "Golden Bible," as it was called, while awaiting their return. What happened is described in an account appearing in Andrew Jenson's Latter-day Saint Biographical Encyclopedia.

* * *

The neighbors, who often came in and heard portions of it read, ridiculed it and offered many objections to its contents. These young George A. soon found himself trying to answer, and although he professed no belief in the book himself, having in fact noted many serious objections to it, he was so success-ful in refuting the charges the neighbors brought against it that they generally turned from the argument discomfited, with the observation to his mother that her boy was a little too smart for them. When his uncle and Don Carlos returned, George A. laid before them his objections, which he believed to be unanswer-able. His uncle took them up carefully, quoted the Scriptures upon the subject, showed the reasonableness of the record, and was so successful as to entirely remove every objection, and to convince him that it was just what it purported to be. George A. from that time ever after advocated the divine authenticity of the Book of Mormon. He was also convinced of the necessity of religion, and not being sufficiently instructed by his relatives how to obtain it, after they had left, he attended a protracted series of Congregational revival meetings. These lasted seven-teen days, and effected the "conversion of every sinner in Pots-dam" who attended them except George A., who went to the meeting regularly, sat in the gallery listening attentively, but waited in vain for the sensation of religion which should bring him down to the anxious bench. Finally, prayers and exhorta-tions having failed, the minister, Rev. Frederick E. Cannon, pronounced him reprobate and sealed him up unto eternal damnation, saying, "Thy blood be upon thine own head!" Nine times he thus delivered this inoffensive but unsatisfied seeker for religion to the buffetings of Satan and the burning of an endless hell. For two years George A. had performed the greater part of the labor on his father's farm, but in the winter of 1832-33, he attended school, and gave considerable attention to studying the gospel and its requirements. He was baptized by Joseph H. Wakefield Sept. 10, 1832. (From Jenson 1:38.)

Daniel Spencer, Jr.

Daniel Spencer, Jr., son of Daniel Spencer, Sr., and Chloe Wilson, was born on 20 July 1794 in West Stockbridge, Berk-shire, Massachusetts. From 1815 to 1828, he was the owner and proprietor of a successful mercantile house in Savannah, Georgia. At the close of his commercial career in the South, he re-turned to West Stockbridge and married Sophronia Eliza Pomeroy. They became the parents of one child. Daniel soon en-tered into partnership with marble dealers in the Stockbridge community: "So much trusted by the firm was he that the whole supervision of the firm fell upon his shoulders" (Jenson 1:287).

It was not until 1840 that Daniel read the Book of Mormon. A prayerful search of its contents led to his baptism and subsequent move to Nauvoo, Illinois, where he served as the mayor after the death of the Prophet Joseph Smith. From 1849 to 1868 he was president of the Salt Lake Stake. Daniel died on 8 December 1868 in Salt Lake City at the age of seventy-four.

An account in Jenson's Latter-day Saint Biographical Encyclopedia details his conversion to The Church of Jesus Christ of Latter-day Saints.

*   *   *

Until 1840 no Elder of the Mormon Church had preached in [Daniel's] native town. The late John Van Cott, however, belonged to the same region, and already his relatives, the Pratts, had been laboring to impress Mr. Van Cott with the "Mormon" faith. But Daniel Spencer, up to this date, had no relationship whatever with the people with whom himself and his brother Orson afterwards became so prominently identified. At this time Daniel Spencer belonged to no sect of religionists, but sustained in the community the name of a man marked for character and moral worth. It was, however, his custom to give free quarters to preachers of all denominations. The "Mormon" Elder came; and his coming created an epoch in Daniel Spencer's life. Through his influence the Presbyterian meeting house was obtained for the "Mormon" Elder to preach the gospel, and the meeting was attended by the elite of the town. At the close of the service the Elder asked the assembly if there was any one present who would give him "a night's lodging and a meal of victuals in the name of Jesus." For several minutes a dead silence reigned in the congregation. None present seemed desirous to peril their character or taint their respectability by taking home a "Mormon" Elder. At length Daniel Spencer, in the old Puritan spirit and the proud independence so characteristic of the true American gentleman, rose up, stepped into the aisle, and broke the silence: "I will entertain you, sir, for humanity's sake." Daniel took the poor Elder, not to his public hotel, as was his wont with the preachers generally who needed hospitality, but he took him to his own house, a fine family mansion, and the next morning he clothed him from head to foot with a good suit of broad cloth from the shelves of his store. The Elder continued to preach the new and strange

gospel, and brought upon himself much persecution. This pro-
duced upon the mind of Daniel Spencer an extraordinary effect.
Seeing the bitter malevolence from the preachers and the best
of the professing Christians, and being naturally a philosopher
and a judge, he resolved to investigate the cause of this enmity
and unchristianlike manifestation. The result came. It was as
strongly marked as his conduct during the investigation. For
two weeks he closed his establishment, refused to do business
with any one, and shut himself up to study; and there alone
with his God he weighed in the balances of his clear head and
conscientious heart the divine message and found it not want-
ing. One day, when his son was with him in his study, he suddenly burst into a flood of tears, and exclaimed: "My God, the
thing is true, and as an honest man I must embrace it; but it
will cost me all I have got on earth." He had weighed the conse-
quences, but his conscientious mind compelled him to assume
the responsibility and take up the cross. He saw that he must,
in the eyes of friends and townsmen, fall from the social pin-
nacle on which he then stood to that of a despised people. At
mid-day, about three months after the poor "Mormon" Elder
came into the town of West Stockbridge, Daniel Spencer having
issued a public notice to his townsmen that he should be baptized at noon on a certain day, took him by the arm and, not
ashamed, walked through the town taking the route of the
main street to the waters of baptism, followed by hundreds of
his townsmen to the river's bank. The profoundest respect and
quiet were manifested by the vast concourse of witnesses, but
also the profoundest astonishment. It was nothing wonderful
that a despised "Mormon" Elder should believe in Joseph
Smith, but it was a matter of astonishment that a man of
Daniel Spencer's social standing and character should receive
the mission of the Prophet and divinity of the Book of Mormon.
The conversion and conduct of Daniel Spencer carried a deep
and weighty conviction among many good families in the region
around, which, in a few months, resulted in the establishment
of a flourishing branch of the Church. (From Jenson 1:287.)

John Taylor

*John Taylor, son of James Taylor and Agnes Taylor, was
born on 1 November 1808 in Milnthorpe, Westmoreland, En-*

John Taylor

gland. He married Leonora Cannon on 28 January 1833 in Toronto, Canada, and they became the parents of four children. On 9 May 1836 John was baptized in Toronto by Parley P. Pratt. From 1838 to 1880 he served in the Council of the Twelve Apostles. During these years he labored as a missionary in England, Ireland, and France, and edited the Times and Seasons *in Nauvoo and* The Mormon *in New York. From October 1880 to July 1887 he was President of The Church of Jesus Christ of Latterday Saints. John died on 25 July 1887 in Kaysville, Davis, Utah, at the age of seventy-eight.*

John Taylor told of the events leading to his acceptance of the Mormon faith. Central to his conversion was his reading of the Book of Mormon.

* * *

I was living in the city of Toronto, Upper Canada; I was associated with a number of gentlemen in searching the scriptures. Many of us were connected with the Methodist Society; we did not believe their doctrines because they did not accord with scripture. Nevertheless we did not interfere with them; we considered them as near correct as others; we rejected every man's word or writing, and took the Word of God alone; we had continued diligently at this for two years; we made it a rule to receive no doctrine until we could bring no scripture testimony against it. The gentlemen with whom I associated were, many of them, learned and intelligent. We gathered from the scriptures many important truths; we believed in the gathering of Israel, and in the restoration of the ten tribes; we believed that Jesus would come to reign personally on the earth; we gathered from the scriptures that just judgment would overtake the churches of the world, because of their iniquity. We believed that the Gospel which was preached by the apostles was true, and that any departure from that was a departure from the order of God, and that churches having thus departed were consequently corrupt and fallen.

We believed that there ought to be apostles, prophets, evangelists, pastors, and teachers as in former days, and that the gifts of healing and the power of God ought to be associated with the church. We, of course, believed that where these things did not exist there could not be a true church; but we believed that we had no authority ourselves to teach these principles; we were praying men, and asked our Heavenly Father to show us the truth, and we fasted and prayed, that if God had a true church on the earth he would send us a messenger.

About this time Parley P. Pratt called on me with a letter of introduction from a merchant of my acquaintance. I had peculiar feelings on seeing him. I had heard a great many stories of a similar kind to those that you have heard, and I must say that I thought my friend had imposed upon me a little in sending a man of this persuasion to me. I, however, received him courteously as I was bound to do. I told him, however, plainly, my feelings, and that in our researches I wanted no fables; I wished him to confine himself to the scriptures. We talked for three hours or upwards, and he bound me as close to the scriptures as I desired, proving everything he said therefrom. I afterwards wrote down eight sermons that he preached in order that I might compare them with the word of God. I found nothing contrary.

I then examined the Book of Mormon, and the prophecies concerning that; that was also correct. I then read the book of "Doctrine and Covenants", found nothing unscriptural there. He called upon us to repent and be baptized for the remission of sins, and we should receive the Holy Ghost. But what is that? we inquired; the same, he answered, as it was in the Apostles' days, or nothing. A number of others and myself were baptized, and we realized those blessings according to his word; the gifts and power of God were in the church, the gift of tongues and prophecy; the sick were healed, and we rejoiced in the blessings and gifts of the Holy Ghost. (From "Three Nights' Public Discussion" 17-18.)

Lorenzo Dow Young

Lorenzo Dow Young, son of John Young and Abigail Howe, was born on 19 October 1807 in Smyrna, Chenango, New York. He married Persis Goodall on 6 June 1826 in Watertown, New York, and they became the parents of ten children. In 1831 Lorenzo was baptized by John P. Greene and soon moved to Ohio to be with others of his faith. He suffered persecution in Ohio, Missouri, and Illinois, before fleeing to the Salt Lake Valley. From 1851 to 1878 he served as bishop of the Salt Lake City 18th Ward. Lorenzo died on 21 November 1895 in Salt Lake City at the age of eighty-eight.

In his personal narrative, Lorenzo penned an inspiring account of his first defense of the Book of Mormon and the events that led to his conversion. He displayed his moral integrity throughout his search for truth and his hope for religious joy.

* * *

In the fall of 1828, I returned to Hector, Schuyler County, New York. Quite a number of people lived there of the Campbel lite faith. 'Squire Chase, a prominent man in the neighborhood, who had been a preacher of the sect, said that they were cold in religion and had not held any meetings for several months. I had been there but a few days, when I went with him about two miles to a Methodist meeting. This occurred in the month of November.

Up to this time I had joined no church, although I had professed religion, attended meetings, and preached when I had an opportunity.

On my return, I remarked to Mr. Chase, "Why cannot we have meetings in our neighborhood as well as to go so far to them?"

Lorenzo Dow Young

He replied, "We are all dead there; we would have meetings but I do not feel like preaching. But if you will do the preaching, I will appoint a meeting."

He did so. The first two meetings but few attended. The third meeting the house was crowded. Finally, meetings were held nearly every night in the week, and were well attended. A reformation started among the people, and there were quite a number of religious converts. Campbellite principles had long prevailed in the neighborhood. The converts desired baptism, as that was a prominent principle in the Campbellite faith. Mr. Chase urged me to perform the ordinance. I excused myself by telling him that I had never joined any religious denomination, and did not feel authorized to administer it. I finally utterly refused to do so. He then sent forty or fifty miles for Elder Brown, a regular Campbellite preacher.

He came and baptized about sixty converts and organized a branch of the Campbellite church out of the fruits of my labors. He quite exhausted his persuasive powers to induce me to join the Campbellite church, to take a circuit and go to preaching.

I told him I would not preach his doctrines. If I preached at all, I should preach the whole Bible as I understood it.

He said I could do so, for he did not think I would preach anything wrong.

A spirit worked with me to do all the good I could, but not to join any religious denomination. It prevailed within me against all temptation this time. Perhaps the guardian angel, promised by my mother, watched over my spiritual as well as temporal welfare. I think, at the time of this reformation, I had as much of the Spirit of the Lord with me as I could well enjoy in my ignorance of the gospel in its purity. I was full of the testimony of the truth as I understood it.

This reformation in Hector, was a means of temptation to me. I had preached and labored with my might to lead the people to the truth, and Elder Brown had stepped in and reaped the results of my labors. Because I would not join the Campbellite church and preach for them, I was entirely thrown aside. The adversary would reason with me thus: "What is the use of all your preaching? It does not amount to anything to you. You had better attend to your own business and let such nonsense alone."

I listened to these suggestions until I had grieved the Spirit of the Lord which I had enjoyed. I no longer had the Spirit to pray or to exhort the people to lives of righteousness. I was in this condition for several months.

In all this lethargy and darkness, I knew there was such a thing as joy in the Spirit of God—that in the testimony of Jesus there was light and peace. I knew I had accepted a mission to bear this testimony while I should remain on the earth.

Knowing these things, I became, in time, alarmed at my condition, I feared that the Lord had forsaken me. I humbled myself before Him in fasting and prayer. I promised Him that if He would return His good Spirit, I would never again reject its suggestions.

Matters continued thus with me for several weeks. In one of my seasons of prayer and supplication, I sensibly felt that I was again visited by the Holy Spirit. I was encouraged to resume my labors in exhorting the people whenever an opportunity was presented. I went from home on the Sabbath and held meetings in different places. I was employed in this way when I first saw the Book of Mormon, and when the gospel was preached to me.

This, and other experiences, have convinced me that when we question the Holy Spirit it is likely to be grieved, and leave us to ourselves. Then will our darkness be greater than if we had never enjoyed its influences. Perhaps this incident in my life may suggest wisdom to others.

In November, 1829, I removed to a place called Hector Hill. In February, 1831, my father, my brothers Joseph and Brigham, and Heber C. Kimball came to my house. They brought with them the Book of Mormon. They were on their way to visit some Saints in Pennsylvania. Through fear of being deceived, I was quite cautious in religious matters. I read and compared the Book of Mormon with the Bible, and fasted and prayed that I might come to a knowledge of the truth. The Spirit seemed to say, "This is the way; walk ye in it." This was all the testimony I could get at the time; it was not altogether satisfactory.

The following May, Elder Levi Gifford came into the neighborhood, and desired to preach. My brother, John, belonged to the Methodist church, and had charge of their meeting house which was in the neighborhood. I obtained from him permission for Elder Gifford to preach in it. The appointment was circulated for a meeting the same evening.

This was on Saturday evening, and the circuit preacher of that district was to hold a meeting there on Sunday. Elder Midbury, the circuit preacher, attended the meeting. The house was crowded. As soon as Elder Gifford had concluded his discourse, Elder Midbury arose to his feet and said: "Brethren, sisters and friends: I have been a preacher of the gospel for twenty-two years; I do not know that I have been the means of converting a sinner, or reclaiming a poor backslider; but this I do know, that the doctrine the stranger has preached to us tonight is a deception, that Joe Smith is a false prophet, and that the Book of Mormon is from hell."

After talking awhile in this strain, he concluded. I immediately arose to my feet and asked the privilege of speaking, which was granted. I said that Elder Midbury, in his remarks, entirely ignored the possibility of more revelation, and acknowledged that he had been a preacher of the gospel for twenty-two years, without knowing that he had been the means of converting a sinner, or of reclaiming a poor backslider. But still he claimed to know that the doctrine he had just heard was false, that Joseph Smith was an impostor, and that the Book of Mormon was from hell. "Now, how is it possible," I asked, "for him to know these things unless he has received a revelation?"

When I sat down a strong man, by the name of Thompson,

who was well known in the neighborhood as a beligerent character, stepped up to Elder Gifford and demanded the proofs of the authenticity of the Book of Mormon.

Elder Gifford replied, "I have said all I care about saying tonight."

Then said Mr. Thompson, "we will take the privilege of clothing you with a coat of tar and feathers, and riding you out of town on a rail."

In the meantime, four or five others of like character came to the front.

Acting under the impulse of the moment—true to the instincts of my nature to protect the weak against the strong, I stepped between Elder Gifford and Mr. Thompson. Looking the latter in the eye, I said, "Mr. Thompson, you cannot lay your hand on this stranger to harm a hair of his head, without you do it over my dead body."

He replied by mere threats of violence, which brought my brother John to his feet.

With a voice and manner, that carried with it a power greater than I had ever seen manifested in him before, and, I might say, since, he commanded Mr. Thompson and party to take their seats. He continued, "Gentlemen, if you offer to lay a hand on Mr. Gifford, you shall pass through my hands, after which I think you will not want any more to-night." Mr. Thompson and party quieted down and then took their seats.

Since then the Elders have passed through so many similar experiences, that they have ceased to be a novelty. That there should be such a powerful antagonism of spirits manifesting themselves in muscle, in a Christian church, indicated a new era in religious influences. (From "Lorenzo Dow Young's Narrative" 31-35.)

Phinehas Howe Young

Phinehas Howe Young, son of John Young and Abigail Howe, was born on 16 February 1799 in Hopkinton, Middlesex, Massachusetts. He married Clarissa Hamilton on 18 January 1818 in Auburn, New York, and they became the parents of two children. In 1824 Phinehas joined the Methodist Church and began preaching in Canada and the United States. After six years in the ministry, he was visited by Samuel Smith, the first

Phinehas Howe Young

missionary to carry a Book of Mormon. Through Samuel's urging, Phinehas read the book and on 5 April 1832 accepted baptism. He served missions in Canada, Virginia, New York, Ohio, and England. From 1864 to 1871 he was bishop of the Salt Lake City 2nd Ward. Phinehas died on 10 October 1879 in Salt Lake City at the age of eighty.

S. Dilworth Young, a descendant of Phinehas's brother Joseph, wrote of Phinehas's meeting with Samuel Smith and of his first impression of the Book of Mormon. This descriptive narrative was based on Phinehas's personal writings and vividly portrays the character of both the first missionary and the potential convert. The common ground for each man proved to be the Book of Mormon.

✳ ✳ ✳

Phinehas Howe Young rode through the woods one spring day in 1830 with joy in his heart. The first faint green of growing things was beginning to show against the browns and greys of retreating winter. He had been preaching the evening before at Lima, a distance through the woods of seven or eight miles to the south. The folks had received him well so there was reason to feel glad; God had been good to him, he felt. It was nearly noon when he stopped at the Tomlinson farm to obtain dinner. This was common practice for preachers, and for others. If there was a farm handy, come noon, one was welcome to sit up and eat, even though he might be a stranger to the farmers. Phinehas was no stranger to these folks. They had seen his comings and goings and had accepted his idea of religion; he knew he would be welcome.

He began exchanging with the family the small gossip that holds communities together with its fine web of rumor, truth, and wit, when there was an interruption. A young man, dressed in the rough homespun clothes of the frontier, came into the room and singled out Phinehas. He had an open, frank face, and his speech was slow and studied; apparently it was not easy for him to express himself fluently. He held a book in his hand, which he offered to Phinehas.

"There's a book, sir, I wish you to read."

Phinehas hesitated: "Pray, sir, what book have you?"

"The Book of Mormon, or, as it is called by some, the Golden Bible."

"Ah, so then it purports to be a revelation?"

"Yes, a revelation from God."

The young man showed Phinehas the last two pages of the book.

"Here is the testimony of the witness to the truth of the Book."

Phinehas read the testimony of three witnesses, which said they had seen the plates from which the book had been translated, that an angel had shown these plates to them and that a voice had declared it to be true. Then he read the testimony of eight others which stated that they had been shown the plates by the "said Smith" and that they had "hefted" them; further, that the plates and the engravings on them appeared to be of "curious workmanship."

The young man continued: "If you will read this book with a prayerful heart and ask God to give you a witness, you will know the truth of the work."

His earnest demeanor and forthright manner impressed Phinehas who told the young man he would certainly read it. Phinehas asked him his name.

"My name is Samuel H. Smith."

"Then you are one of the witnesses."

"Yes, I know the book is a revelation from God, translated by the power of the Holy Ghost, and that my brother, Joseph Smith, Jr., is a Prophet, Seer, and Revelator."

To Phinehas this was strange language. But he bought the copy and promised to read the book. The conversation shifted to other matters, and soon after dinner they parted, each to go his separate way. The more Phinehas considered, the more he felt that Samuel H. Smith was deceived, that the book was written to deceive people; therefore as minister of a flock he had a duty to expose the deception to the people and save them from its errors. On his arrival home in Victor, six miles from Mendon, that afternoon he said to Clarissa, his wife: "I have got a week's work laid out, and hope that nothing will occur to prevent my accomplishing the task."

"Have you anything new to attend to?" she asked.

"I have got a book here called the Book of Mormon, and it is said to be a revelation, and I wish to read it and make myself acquainted with its errors, so I can expose them to the world."

He read the book during the week, then read it again the following week. To his surprise he could not find the anticipated errors, but felt, rather, a conviction that what he had been reading was true. The next Sabbath he was asked by the congregation to give his views on the book. He defended it for ten minutes, when suddenly the Spirit of God came on him with such force that in a marvelous manner he spoke at great length on the importance of it, quoting copiously from the Bible to support his position. He closed by telling the people that he believed the book. (From Young 50-52.)

4

A Testimony Worth Defending

A testimony worth having is a testimony worth defending. The actions of Mother Smith, Father Smith, Emma Hale Smith, Oliver Cowdery, David Whitmer, and other early Latter-day Saints affirm this belief. Each stood firm in his or her testimony of the Book of Mormon, defending it whenever necessary against enemies or friends, critics or sympathizers.

Lucy Mack Smith

"I Know It to Be True"

While Oliver Cowdery was copying the original Book of Mormon manuscript, Palmyra citizens were plotting to hinder its publication. Three men determined they would visit the Smith home when Father Smith and his sons were absent and entreat Lucy to display the manuscript. Two of them would divert her attention, and the third would snatch the manuscript and throw it into the fire. The conspirators concluded that if this plot failed, they would swear never to purchase a copy of the Book of Mormon or permit any of their family members to read it.

Four days after the clandestine council, the three purportedly respectable members of the Palmyra community came to visit Mother Smith. Finding the men absent, as they had planned, they asked: "Mrs. Smith, we hear that you have a gold bible; we have come to see if you will be so kind as to show it to us?" As she relates in her account, Lucy responded not in fear, but determination:

> "No, gentlemen," said I, "we have no gold bible, but we have a translation of some gold plates, which have been brought forth for the purpose of making known to the world the plainness of the gospel, and also to give a history of the people which formerly inhabited this continent." (*History of Joseph Smith* 160.)

Lucy spoke of the gospel principles contained in the Book of Mormon. She endeavored to explain the similarities between the Book of Mormon and the New Testament, treating the three men as potential converts.

Deacon Beckwith, the religious spokesman of the conspirators, lamented: "Mrs. Smith, you and the most of your children have belonged to our church for some length of time, and we respect you very highly. You say a good deal about the Book of Mormon. . . . I wish, that if you do believe those things, you would not say anything more upon the subject." Recognizing this calculated rebuke, Lucy unwaveringly declared her right to speak of the Book of Mormon: " 'Deacon Beckwith,' said I, 'if you should stick my flesh full of faggots, and even burn me at the stake, I would declare, as long as God should give me breath, that Joseph has got that Record, and that I know it to be true.' " (*History of Joseph Smith* 161.)

"Is the Book of Mormon True?"

In obedience to the revelation to gather to Ohio, eighty faithful Saints congregated at the Smith home in 1831 to bid farewell to family and friends remaining in the New York area. Mother Smith joined the embarking Saints on a small boat on the Erie Canal near Waterloo, New York. Aboard the vessel, the new converts sang hymns of praise to God. Their singing so delighted the captain that he called to his mate, saying, "Do, come here, and steer the boat; for I must hear that singing" (qtd. in Lucy Mack Smith, *History of Joseph Smith* 196).

When the emigrants arrived in Buffalo, New York, five days after their departure, they met a group of Saints who had journeyed from Colesville, New York. Lucy asked the Colesville members if they had confessed to the townspeople of Buffalo that they were Mormons. "No, indeed," they said, "neither must you mention a word about your religion, for if you do you will never be able to get a house, or a boat either." Lucy described her response: "I told them I should tell the people precisely who I was; 'and . . . if you are ashamed of Christ, you must not expect to be prospered; and I shall wonder if we do not get to Kirtland before you.' " (*History of Joseph Smith* 199.)

Blocks of ice impeded travel on the Erie Canal. Small and large boats hugged the shoreline as captains slowly maneuvered their crafts through the ice-packed waterway. While waiting for a break in the ice, Mother Smith was hailed by a man on the shore who hollered, "Is the Book of Mormon true?" She did not hesitate in her reply:

> "That book," replied I, "was brought forth by the power of God, and translated by the gift of the Holy Ghost; and, if I could make my voice sound as loud as the trumpet of Michael, the Archangel, I would declare the truth from land to land, and from sea to sea, and the echo should reach to every isle, until every member of the family of Adam should be left without excuse." (*History of Joseph Smith* 204.)

She further testified "God has revealed himself to man again in these last days." She warned the inquisitive man: "[God] has commenced a work which will prove a savor of life unto life, or of death unto death, to every one that stands here this day—of life unto life—if you will receive it, or of death unto death, if you reject the counsel of God." (*History of Joseph Smith* 204.)

After responding to the man's query, Lucy turned to the Saints and asked them to pray that the ice would break so they could continue their journey to Ohio. At that instant, a noise like thunder was heard. The ice jam opened up long enough for Lucy's boat to pass through, and then closed again, leaving the hesitant Colesville Saints behind in Buffalo.

Joseph Smith, Sr.

"You Are My Prisoner"

As proselyting efforts increased in 1830, Joseph, Hyrum, Samuel, and other members of the Smith household often traveled throughout the countryside preaching of the Restoration. Father and Mother Smith and young Lucy were often left alone in their Palmyra home. One Wednesday morning Father Smith arose from his bed feeling ill and tense because of the growing religious persecution in the neighborhood. While Lucy was preparing milk porridge for his nourishment, a Quaker stopped by and confronted him. "Friend Smith," he stated in traditional Quaker terms, "I have a note against thee for fourteen dollars, which I have lately bought, and I have come to see if thou hast the money for me" (qtd. in Lucy Mack Smith, *History of Joseph Smith* 179).

Father Smith asked the Quaker why he had purchased the note, as he was obviously not in need of money. The Quaker, knowing that Joseph did not possess the funds necessary to redeem the note, answered, "That is business of my own; I want the money, and must have it." Father Smith then offered to pay six dollars in cash and procure the rest later, but the Quaker would not be satisfied by these terms. He refused all reasonable offers of payment, including Lucy's gold beads. He exclaimed:

> "No, I will not wait one hour; and if thou dost not pay me immediately, thou shalt go forthwith to the jail, unless (running to the fireplace and making violent gestures with his hands towards the fir [fire]) thou wilt burn up those Books of Mormon; but if thou wilt burn them up, then I will forgive thee the whole debt." (Qtd. in Lucy Mack Smith, *History of Joseph Smith* 179-80.)

Father Smith refused to burn even one copy of the Book of Mormon. "Then, thou shalt go to jail," the Quaker declared. He stepped to the door and called to the waiting constable, who laid his hands on Father Smith's shoulder and said, "You are my prisoner." Joseph Smith, Sr., was forced to sit in the burning sun, faint with hunger and sick with the night's illness, while the Quaker stood guard over him. The constable returned to the house and ate the food Mother Smith had prepared for her husband. (Lucy Mack Smith, *History of Joseph Smith* 180-81.)

Joseph endured the privations of exposure and jail rather than burn one copy of the Book of Mormon. When his son, Samuel, came to visit him after four days of confinement, Father Smith said:

> "Immediately after I left your mother, the men by whom I was taken commenced using every possible argument to induce me to renounce the Book of Mormon, saying, 'how much better it would be for you to deny that silly thing, than to be disgraced and imprisoned, when you might not only escape this, but also have the note back, as well as the money which you have paid on it.' To this I made no reply. . . . I thought to myself, I was not the first man who had been imprisoned for the truth's sake; and when I should meet Paul in the Paradise of God, I could tell him that I, too, had been in bonds for the Gospel which he had preached." (Qtd. in Lucy Mack Smith, *History of Joseph Smith* 185.)

Emma Hale Smith

"I Am Satisfied"

In 1827, the young bride, Emma Smith, waited in a wagon at the bottom of the Hill Cumorah for her husband to return with the gold plates. This was her first contact with the sacred book. During the half century that followed, she endured persecution and trials because of her faith in the Book of Mormon and her belief in the prophetic calling of her husband.

On 14 February 1879, two months before her death and fifty-two years since her initial knowledge of the Book of Mormon, Joseph Smith III, her oldest living son, approached her bedside to inquire of her testimony of the Book of Mormon. During his series of questions, Emma declared:

> The Book of Mormon is of divine authenticity—I have not the slightest doubt of it. I am satisfied that no man could have dictated the writing of the manuscripts unless he was inspired; for, when acting as a scribe, your father would dictate to me hour after hour; and when returning after

meals or after interruptions, he would at once begin where he had left off, without either seeing the manuscript or having any portion of it read to him. This was a usual thing for him to do. It would have been improbable that a learned man could do this; and, for one so ignorant and unlearned as he was, it was simply impossible. (Qtd. in Joseph Smith III 52.)

Emma not only attested to the authenticity of the translation in this exacting manner but also described the physical reality of the plates from which the Book of Mormon was translated:

The plates often lay on the table without any attempt at concealment, wrapped in a small linen table cloth, which I had given him to fold them in. I once felt of the plates as they thus lay on the table, tracing their outline and shape. They seemed to be pliable like thick paper, and would rustle with a metallic sound when the edges were moved by the thumb, as one does sometimes thumb the edges of a book. (Qtd in Joseph Smith III 289-90.)

Sidney Rigdon

"I Can Swear Before High Heaven"

Shortly after Sidney Rigdon joined the Church and traveled to western New York to meet the Prophet Joseph Smith, critics accused him of being the author of the Book of Mormon. For decades many of Joseph Smith's enemies refused to believe the origin of the Book of Mormon as professed by the Prophet and concluded instead that the religiously inclined Sidney Rigdon was the logical author.

In 1865, twenty-one years after the death of Joseph Smith and Sidney's excommunication, Sidney's son, John Wickliffe Rigdon, asked his father about this rumored authorship. Challenging his father, he said: "You have been charged with writing that book and giving it to Joseph Smith to introduce to the world. You have always told me one story; that you never saw the book until it was presented to you by Parley P. Pratt and Oliver Cowdery; and all you ever knew of the origin of that book was what they told you and what Joseph Smith and the witnesses who claimed to have seen the plates had told you. Is this true? If so, all right; if it is not, you owe it to me and your family to tell it." The elderly Sidney raised his hand and said, with tears glistening in his eyes:

> My son, I can swear before high heaven that what I have told you about the origin of that book is true. . . . And in all my intimacy with Joseph Smith he never told me but the one story, and that was that he found it engraved upon gold plates in a hill near Palmyra, New York, and that an angel had appeared to him and directed him where to find it; and I have never, to you or to anyone else, told but the one story, and that I now repeat to you.

John Rigdon reported that his father also said "that 'Mormonism' was true; that Joseph Smith was a Prophet, and this world would find it out some day." (Qtd. in Joseph Smith, *History of the Church* 1:123n.)

Oliver Cowdery

"May It Please the Court"

By the time of his excommunication on 12 April 1838, Oliver Cowdery had made future plans to practice law. He joined his brothers, Warren and Lyman, who were beginning their law careers in Ohio. From 1840 to 1847 Oliver resided in Tiffin, Ohio, where he was a successful attorney and a politician. In 1847 he moved to Elkhorn, Wisconsin, and established a law practice with his brother Lyman. Less than a year after his arrival in Elkhorn, he was nominated to be a state assemblyman. During the election of 1848, campaign smears attempted to link Oliver to Joseph Smith and the origins of the Book of Mormon.

Many years later, Judge C. M. Nielsen of Salt Lake City related a story told to him in the year 1884 concerning Oliver's reaction to another attorney's contemptuous charge that he professed to have seen the plates from which the Book of Mormon was translated. According to this account, Oliver Cowdery answered:

May it please the court and the gentlemen of the jury, my brother attorney on the other side has charged me with connection with Joseph Smith and the golden Bible. The responsibility has been placed upon me, and I cannot escape reply. . . . Before God and man I dare not deny what I have said, and what my testimony contains and as written and printed on the front page of the Book of Mormon. May it please your honor and gentlemen of the jury, this I say, I saw the angel and heard his voice—how can I deny it? It happened in the day time when the sun was shining bright in the firmament; not in the night when I was asleep. That glorious messenger from heaven dressed in white, standing above the ground, in a glory, I have never seen anything to compare, with the sun insignificant in comparison, . . . told us if we denied that testimony there is no forgiveness in this life nor in the world to come. Now how can I deny it—I dare not; I will not. (Qtd. in Gunn 199-200.)

"I Wrote with My Own Pen"

After eleven years' absence from friends and affiliations with The Church of Jesus Christ of Latter-day Saints, Oliver Cowdery desired to return to full fellowship. In 1848 he and his family left their home in Elkhorn, Wisconsin, and journeyed to Kanesville, Iowa, where the Saints had gathered in a temporary encampment. On 21 October 1848, Oliver addressed a conference of the Church:

My name is Cowdery—Oliver Cowdery. In the history of the Church I stood identified with him [Joseph Smith], and was in her councils not because I was better than other men was I called to fill the purposes of God. He called me to a high and holy calling. I wrote with my own pen the entire Book of Mormon (save a few pages) as it fell from the lips of the Prophet Joseph Smith, and he translated it by the power and gift of God, by means of the Urim and Thummim, or as it is called by that book, 'Holy Interpreters'.

I beheld with my eyes and handled with my hands, the gold plates from which it was translated. I also saw with my eyes and handled with my hands, the 'Holy Interpreters'. That book is true, Sidney Rigdon did not write it; Mr. Spaulding did not write it; I wrote it myself as it fell from the lips of the Prophet. It contains the everlasting Gospel, to preach to every nation, kindred, tongue and people. It contains principles of Salvation, and if you my hearers, will walk by its light, and obey its precepts, you will be saved with an everlasting salvation in the Kingdom of God. (Qtd. in Gunn 203-4.)

A few days later, Oliver approached the Kanesville high council and formally requested Church membership. The council considered his request, and, upon the motion of branch president Orson Hyde, Oliver's full fellowship was granted. He was rebaptized on 12 November 1848 in the Missouri River.

David Whitmer

"He Did Hear the Voice of God"

David Whitmer, one of the three witnesses of the Book of Mormon, was a key figure in the formative years of The Church of Jesus Christ of Latter-day Saints. He served a number of short missions to New York, Michigan, and Missouri before leaving the Church in 1838. From 1838 until his death on 25 January 1888, David resided in Richmond, Missouri, living "without stain or blemish" (*Richmond Conservator*). He enjoyed the "confidence and esteem of his fellow men," and was elected to the city council and to the office of mayor (*Richmond Democrat*).

David was the most frequently interviewed witness of the Book of Mormon. One of those who interviewed him was young James H. Moyle, a law student whose account of visiting the gray-haired witness in 1885 was recorded by President David O. McKay. Upon arriving at David Whitmer's home, Moyle explained that he had come to inquire about his testimony published in the Book of Mormon:

He [Whitmer] told me in all the solemnity of his advanced years, that the testimony he had given to the world, and which was published in the Book of Mormon, was true, every word of it, and that he had never deviated or departed in any particular from that testimony, and that nothing in the world could separate him from the sacred message that was delivered to him (qtd. in McKay 89).

Moyle wondered if it were possible that David had been deceived, and questioned him as to whether some psychological
factors could have falsely convinced him. He then persuaded
David to relate every detail of his witness of the Book of Mormon:

> He [Whitmer] described minutely the spot in the woods,
> the large log that separated him from the angel, and that he
> saw the plates from which the Book of Mormon was trans-
> lated, that he handled them, and that he did hear the voice
> of God declare that the plates were correctly translated. . . .
> . . . He said he knew Joseph Smith was a prophet of
> God, and that through him had been restored the gospel of
> Jesus Christ in these latter days. (Qtd. in McKay 89.)

For James Moyle, this firm testimony dispelled all doubt that
David Whitmer had been deceived.

Hyrum Smith

"I Can Assure My Beloved Brethen"

In December 1839, Hyrum Smith wrote a letter entitled, "To
the Saints scattered abroad, Greeting." This letter contains his
testimony of the Book of Mormon and tells of his suffering in
the state of Missouri. Hyrum desired to strengthen his "beloved
brethren" so that they would then know of his continuing "testimony to the world of the truth of the Book of Mormon," despite
his afflictions. A portion of Hyrum's letter reads:

> I had been abused and thrust into a dungeon, and con-
> fined for months on account of my faith, and the testimony
> of Jesus Christ. However I thank God that I felt a determi-
> nation to die, rather than deny the things which my eyes
> had seen, which my hands had handled, and which I had
> borne testimony to . . . ; and I can assure my beloved
> brethren that I was enabled to bear as strong a testimony,
> when nothing but death presented itself, as ever I did in my
> life. My confidence in God, was likewise unshaken. I knew

that He who suffered me, along with my brethren, to be thus tried, that He could and that He would deliver us out of the hands of our enemies; and in His own due time He did so, for which I desire to bless and praise His holy name. (Qtd. in Joseph Smith, *History of the Church* 4:46n.)

Orson Pratt

"I Could Be a Witness Myself"

Orson Pratt was baptized into the Church by his brother, Parley P. Pratt, after reading the Book of Mormon. He became a close associate of the Prophet Joseph Smith and an original member of the Quorum of the Twelve, in which he served for over a total of forty-five years. He filled many missions in the United States, Canada, and Europe, crossing the Atlantic Ocean more than a dozen times to share the restored gospel. On 21 September 1879, Orson Pratt delivered a discourse in the Salt Lake Tabernacle entitled, "The Book of Mormon: An Authentic Record." In his address, he explained the key to gaining a witness of the Book of Mormon and of Joseph Smith's divine calling:

The very message itself in the book, and in the New Testament, and in the modern revelations that are given through the prophet, told me, told you, told all the people upon the face of this earth, how they also might obtain a knowledge of the truth of the Book of Mormon and of this work. . . . If the people of all the nations of the earth will repent, turn unto him [the Lord] and obey his commandments . . . they should receive the Holy Ghost. Will that give us a knowledge as clear, as definite, as pointed as could be revealed by the ministration of angels? Yes. (*Journal of Discourses* 21:175-76.)

Orson then affirmed that he had received his witness of the Book of Mormon from the Holy Ghost. He concluded that the Lord fulfilled his promise, and since that time, he said, "I could be a witness myself" (*Journal of Discourses* 21:176).

Joseph Smith, Jr.

"Brother Joseph Arose like a Lion"

During a trip back East in the latter part of 1839 and early part of 1840, Joseph Smith, Sidney Rigdon, and others spent some time in Philadelphia, Pennsylvania, preaching the gospel and making visits. On one occasion a large church hall was opened to the Prophet, and three thousand people gathered to hear his words. Sidney Rigdon spoke first and, hoping either not to offend the audience or to reach them at their level of understanding, introduced the gospel in terms of the Bible only. Joseph did not mince words but commenced his address by defending the Book of Mormon. Parley P. Pratt commented on this incident:

> Brother Joseph arose like a lion about to roar; and being full of the Holy Ghost, spoke in great power, bearing testimony of the visions he had seen, the ministering of angels which he had enjoyed; and how he had found the plates of the Book of Mormon, and translated them by the gift and power of God. He commenced by saying: "If nobody else had the courage to testify of so glorious a message from Heaven, and of the finding of so glorious a record, he felt to do it in justice to the people, and leave the event with God." (260.)

During his trip back East, the Prophet also spent time in Washington, D.C. A report of a discourse he gave there states that Joseph declared that the Book of Mormon was "communicated to him, *direct from heaven.* . . . He had penned it as dictated by God." (*Words of Joseph Smith* 34, emphasis in original.)

"God Is the Author of It"

Joseph's unwavering defense of the Book of Mormon caused him continual persecution. Nevertheless, on 12 February 1834, he confidently proclaimed at a priesthood meeting in Kirtland, Ohio: "I [will] stand and shine like the sun in the firmament, when my enemies and the gainsayers of my testimony shall be put down and cut off, and their names blotted out from among men" (*History of the Church* 2:26). Five years later, in a letter dated 20 March 1839, Joseph and his fellow prisoners in Liberty Jail testified in a letter to the membership of the Church at Quincy, Illinois, and to the Saints scattered abroad: "The Bible is true . . . the Book of Mormon is true" (*Personal Writings of Joseph Smith* 407).

Although persecuted, mocked, and despised for his stand on all facets of the Book of Mormon, Joseph did not fear his enemies. He wrote from Liberty Jail: "Hell may pour forth its rage like the burning lava of Mount Vesuvius, or of Etna . . . yet shall 'Mormonism' stand. Water, fire, truth and God are all realities. Truth is 'Mormonism.' God is the author of it. . . . It was by Him we received the Book of Mormon." (*Teachings of the Prophet Joseph Smith* 139.)

"A Powerful Testimony"

About nine o'clock in the evening on 26 June 1844, while confined in Carthage Jail, Joseph listened to his brother Hyrum read of the imprisonment and deliverance of the servants of God as told in the Book of Mormon. After Hyrum's recital and commentary, "Joseph bore a powerful testimony to the guards of the divine authenticity of the Book of Mormon" (*Teachings of the Prophet Joseph Smith* 383).

The Prophet's most complete testimony occurred on the following day. On 27 June 1844 in Carthage, Illinois, Joseph and his brother Hyrum sealed with their blood their own testimonies of the truthfulness of the Book of Mormon. Their assassins left behind much more than the corpses of two men—they left "a broad seal affixed to 'Mormonism' that cannot be rejected by any court on earth" (D&C 135:7). With senseless brutality, the mob forged two martyrs' crowns, unwittingly verifying the "truth of the everlasting gospel that all the world cannot impeach" (D&C 135:7).

The testators are dead, yet their testament lives on. Joseph's words act as a seal affixed to the truthfulness of the Book of Mormon. Joseph's courageous, constant testimony, unmitigated by any of his words or his deeds, stands firm in its defense and advocacy of the Book of Mormon. Elder John Taylor wrote of the Prophet's death: "The reader in every nation will be reminded that the Book of Mormon . . . cost the best blood of the nineteenth century to bring [it] forth for the salvation of a ruined world" (D&C 135:6).

Bibliography

Sources used from the Archives Division, Church Historical Department, The Church of Jesus Christ of Latter-day Saints, Salt Lake City, Utah (hereafter cited as LDS Church Archives), are used with permission.

Backman, Milton V., Jr., comp. *Writings of Early Latter-day Saints and Their Contemporaries: A Data Base Collection.* Provo, Utah: Religious Studies Center, Brigham Young University, 1991.

Benson, Ezra Taft. "Flooding the Earth with the Book of Mormon." *Ensign* 18 (November 1988): 4-6.

Black, Susan Easton. *Membership of The Church of Jesus Christ of Latter-day Saints, 1830-1848.* 50 vols. Salt Lake City: Corporation of the President of The Church of Jesus Christ of Latter-day Saints, 1990.

Brown, Benjamin. *Testimonies for the Truth. . . .* Liverpool: S. W. Richards, 1853.

Burgess, Harrison. Autobiography. LDS Church Archives.

Carter, Jared. Journal [ca. 1833]. LDS Church Archives.

Chamberlain, Solomon. Autobiography [ca. 1858]. LDS Church Archives.

Cook, Lyndon W. *The Revelations of the Prophet Joseph Smith: A Historical and Biographical Commentary of the Doctrine and Covenants.* Provo, Utah: Seventy's Mission Bookstore, 1981.

Cowley, Matthias F. *Wilford Woodruff: History of His Life and Labors.* 1909. Reprint. Salt Lake City: Bookcraft, 1964.

Crocheron, Augusta Joyce. *Representative Women of Deseret.* Salt Lake City: J. C. Graham and Co., 1884.

Evans, Beatrice Cannon, and Jonathan Russel Cannon, eds. *Cannon Family Historical Treasury.* Salt Lake City: George Cannon Family Association, 1967.

Evans, John Henry. *Charles Coulson Rich: Pioneer Builder of the West.* New York: Macmillan, 1936.

Fletcher, Rupert J., and Daisy Whiting Fletcher. *Alpheus Cutler and the Church of Christ.* Independence, Mo.: Church of Jesus Christ, 1974.

Green, Forace, comp. *Testimonies of Our Leaders.* Salt Lake City: Bookcraft, 1958.

Gunn, Stanley R. *Oliver Cowdery: Second Elder and Scribe.* Salt Lake City: Bookcraft, 1962.

Hurd, Jerrie W. *Our Sisters in the Latter-day Scriptures.* Salt Lake City: Deseret Book Co., 1987.

Hyde, Orson. Autobiography. Harold B. Lee Library, Brigham Young University, Provo, Utah.

Jenson Andrew. *Latter-day Saint Biographical Encyclopedia.* 4 vols. 1901-36. Reprint. Salt Lake City: Western Epics, 1971.

Johnson, Benjamin F. *My Life's Review.* Independence, Mo.: Zion's Printing and Publishing Co., 1947.

Johnson, Joel Hills. Autobiography. Harold B. Lee Library, Brigham Young University, Provo, Utah.

Journal of Discourses. 26 vols. London: Latter-day Saints' Book Depot, 1854-86.

Judd, Mary Grant. "Rachel Ridgway Ivins Grant." *Relief Society Magazine* 30 (April 1943): 227-31, 297.

Little, James A. *Jacob Hamblin.* 1881. Reprinted in *Three Mormon Classics,* compiled by Preston Nibley, pp. 197-349. Salt Lake City: Bookcraft, 1988.

"Lorenzo Dow Young's Narrative." In *Fragments of Experience,* pp. 22-54. Salt Lake City: Juvenile Instructor Office, 1882.

McKay, David O. *Gospel Ideals: Selections from the Discourses of David O. McKay.* Salt Lake City: Improvement Era, 1953.

"Mary Elizabeth Rollins Lightner." *Utah Genealogical and Historical Magazine* 17 (July 1926): 193-205.

Murdock, John. Journal [ca. 1830-1859]. LDS Church Archives.

Packard, Noah. Autobiography. Harold B. Lee Library, Brigham Young University, Provo, Utah.

Pettegrew, David. Journal. Harold B. Lee Library, Brigham Young University, Provo, Utah.

Phelps, Morris Charles. Autobiography. LDS Church Archives.

Phelps, William W. In *Latter Day Saints' Messenger and Advocate* 1 (September 1835): 177-79.

Pratt, Parley P. *Autobiography of Parley P. Pratt.* Edited by Parley P. Pratt, Jr. 1874. Reprint. Salt Lake City: Deseret Book Co., 1985.

Pulsipher, Zera. Autobiography. Harold B. Lee Library, Brigham Young University, Provo, Utah.

Richmond [Missouri] Conservator, 22 August 1881.

Richmond [Missouri] Democrat, 26 January 1888.

Roberts, B. H. *The Life of John Taylor.* Salt Lake City: Bookcraft, 1963.

Robinson, Ebenezer. *The Return* 2 (1890), 257-62. LDS Church Archives.

Salisbury, Katherine. "Dear Sisters." *Saints' Herald* 33 (1 May 1886): 260.

Shurtliff, Luman Andros. "Biographical Sketch of the Life of Luman Andros Shurtliff." Harold B. Lee Library, Brigham Young University, Provo, Utah.

Smith, George A. Autobiographical record entitled "Memoirs of George A. Smith." George A. Smith Collection. LDS Church Archives.

Smith, Joseph. *History of The Church of Jesus Christ of Latter-day Saints.* Edited by B. H. Roberts. 2d, ed., rev. Salt Lake City: The Church of Jesus Christ of Latter-day Saints, 1932-51.

——. *The Personal Writings of Joseph Smith.* Compiled and edited by Dean C. Jessee. Salt Lake City: Deseret Book Co., 1984.

——. *Teachings of the Prophet Joseph Smith.* Selected by Joseph Fielding Smith. Salt Lake City: Deseret Book Co., 1938.

——. *The Words of Joseph Smith.* Compiled and edited by Andrew F. Ehat and Lyndon W. Cook. Provo, Utah: Religious Studies Center, Brigham Young University, 1980.

Smith, Joseph III. "Last Testimony of Sister Emma." *Saints' Advocate,* 2 October 1879.

Smith, Lucy Mack. *Biographical Sketches of Joseph Smith the Prophet and His Progenitors for Many Generations.* Lamoni,

Iowa: Reorganized Church of Jesus Christ of Latter Day Saints, 1912.

——. *History of Joseph by His Mother.* Edited by Preston Nibley. Salt Lake City: Bookcraft, 1958.

"Statement of Emma Smith to Her Son, Joseph Smith III." *Saints' Herald* 26 (1 October 1879): 289-90.

Talmage, Mary Booth. "Past Three Score Years and Ten." *Young Woman's Journal* 12 (June 1901): 255-57.

"Three Nights' Public Discussion between the Reverends C. W. Cleeve, James Robertson and Philip Carter, and John Taylor of the Church of Jesus Christ of Latter-day Saints, at Boulogne-Sur-Mer, France." *John Taylor's Works.* Harold B. Lee Library, Brigham Young University, Provo, Utah.

Tullidge, Edward W. *The Women of Mormondom.* New York: Tullidge and Crandall, 1877.

Tyler, Daniel. "Incidents of Experience." In *Scraps of Biography,* pp. 20-46. Salt Lake City: Juvenile Instructor Office, 1883.

Young, S. Dilworth. *"Here Is Brigham . . ."* Salt Lake City: Bookcraft, 1964.